JIM MARSHALL

by Leonore Fleischer

JONI MITCHELL

NEW YORK *Flash Books* LONDON

International Standard Book Number: 0-8256-3907-7
Library of Congress Catalog Card Number: 75-29868
Printed in the United States of America.

In Great Britain: Book Sales Ltd., 78 Newman Street, London W1, England.
In Canada: Gage Trade Publishing, P. O. Box 5000, 164 Commander Blvd.,
Agincourt, Ontario M1S 3C7

Designed by Jon Goodchild
Cover photographs by Norman Seeff

Joni Mitchell

The spotlight picks her out on the stage and the fans begin to yell: "JONI! JONI!!" She stands there, smiling shyly, a tall woman with rivers of yellow hair cascading over her shoulders and onto her spangled dress. In her hands she holds a folk guitar; behind her is a piano on which rests a vase of red roses, symbolic of her life and her music. She is Joni Mitchell, artist, writer, composer, singer, superstar, woman of heart and mind.

In the last ten years Joni Mitchell has risen from obscurity to the pinnacle of fame. She has earned a great deal of money, through both her appearances and her recordings. She has tasted the bitterness of notoriety and shrunk away from it. She has withdrawn from the performing stage and then, with renewed courage and energy, she has returned to it. But never, not for one moment, has she stopped writing, not even in the darkest days of depression and loneliness.

Joni's music has brought much gladness to many people. Songs like "Both Sides Now," "Chelsea Morning," "Woodstock," "Help Me," and "The Circle Game" have entered our musical language forever. But

7

Joni Mitchell has paid heavy dues for her success, and has often had to take her freedom at the cost of her happiness. Now she seems to have achieved a large measure of what she has been looking for; her home in Vancouver brings her the solitude she needs to write her music and paint her paintings, while her house in Los Angeles keeps her in the thick of the thriving record business and in touch with the pulsating heart of the music scene.

Who is she, this Magic Princess who has communicated her pilgrimage through the labyrinth of the heart to so many millions by means of her art? A Scorpio, fascinating, magnetic, emotional, creative, vital, and sensual. It is characteristic of Scorpios that their passions are at war with their reason, pulling them into rocky love affairs which prove ultimately disappointing. Life is frequently a battle for Scorpios, as it was for Joni in her scuffling days.

Perhaps the best physical description of Joni was given by Larry LeBlanc in *Rolling Stone* some years ago. He saw Joni Mitchell as "so perfect with high soft cheekbones, great bright blue eyes, bittersweet blonde hair dribbling down past her shoulders; she has a broad smile worth waiting for and a tremendous vanilla grin which makes her always magical."

Her speaking voice is gentle and breathy, tinged with the clean prairie accent of wheatland Canada, her home. Her blonde hair is waist-length, her freckles make her seem much younger than she is, as do her large, wide-apart blue eyes, her chief claim to beauty.

After her concerts, her fans wait for her at the stage door of the theater. They are a quiet group, in the main, filled with love and peace and the plaintive memories of Joni's music. They give her roses, with which she is identified, or, sometimes, she gives *them* roses. They never yell at her, or try to grab her. Instead, they smile and smile, possessed with love.

Joni Mitchell has that effect on people.

CROSBY STILLS NASH and YOUNG

Joni Mitchell '74

HENRY DILTZ

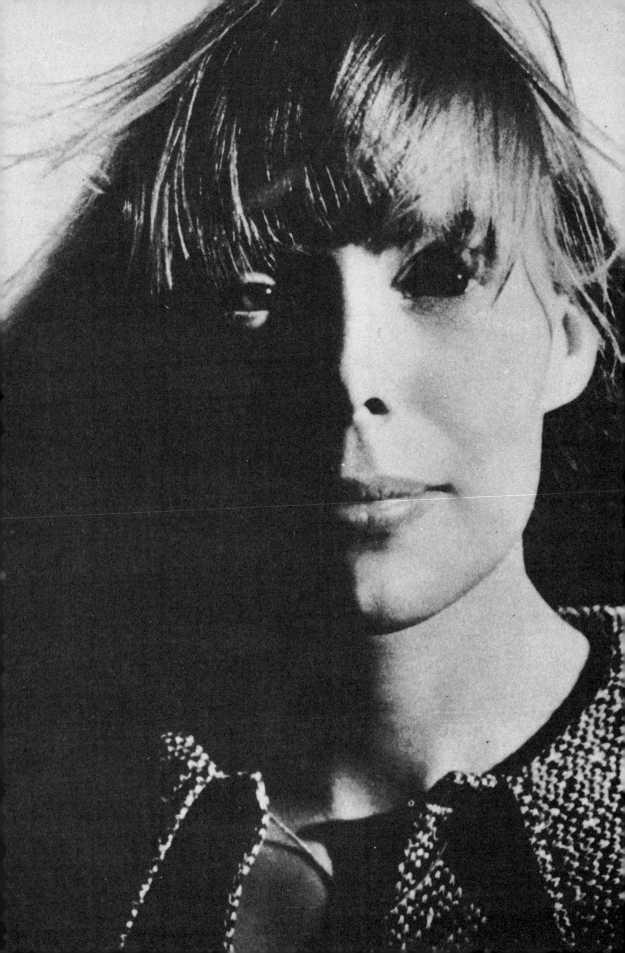

HER LIFE

Fort Macleod, Alberta, is a spot on the map not far north of the Montana-Canada border. There, on November 7, 1943, a tow-headed blue-eyed daughter was born to Bill and Myrtle Anderson. She was named Roberta Joan. World War II was raging in Europe, Africa, and the Orient; Anderson was stationed at Fort Macleod with the Royal Canadian Air Force. He and his wife and baby girl would be moved to other stations further east, to Calgary and, later, to Yorkton in Saskatchewan. When the war ended, the Andersons stayed in Saskatchewan, first in North Battleford, where Joni's father managed a store for a grocery chain and her mother taught school. By the time Joni was six, the Andersons had settled at last, in Saskatoon, in the rolling heart of the Canadian wheat prairie.

"I was born in Fort Macleod Alberta in the foot hills of the Canadian rockies—an area of extreme temperatures and mirages," wrote Joni Mitchell autobiographically more than twenty years later. "When I was two feet off the ground I collected broken glass and cats. When I was three feet off the ground I made drawings of animals and forest fires. When I was four feet off the ground I discovered boys and bicycles. When I was five feet I began to dance to rock 'n' roll and sing the top ten and bawdy service songs around campfires and someone turned me on to Lambert Hendrix [she meant Hendricks, not Jimi] and Ross and Miles Davis and Later Bob Dylan. Through these vertical spurts there was briefly the church choir, grade one piano, bowling, art college, the twist, marriage, runs in the nylons and always romance— extremes in temperatures and mirages."

Saskatoon was where Joni started school, a tall, clear-eyed child of Scotch-Irish ancestry and obvious artistic leanings. At seven, there was a year of piano lessons, and Joni soon showed an aptitude for drawing and painting. Her mother was familiar with the wild flowers and the songs of the birds and taught them to her little girl. "My mother was a romantic," Joni said later. "She encouraged me in old-fashioned things. I used to keep pressed flowers in a scrapbook. In school I scribbled poems on the backs of notebooks when I got bored. It wasn't until junior high school that I began to take poetry seriously." But the creativity was there early, a distillation of her "romantic" mother and her musical father, who played the trumpet.

Years later, in a candid interview in *Maclean's* magazine with her old friend Malka, a Canadian folksinger, Joni recalled those early years when she first showed the creative spark which would later burst into flame and fame.

"I always had star eyes, I think, always interested in glamor. I had one very creative friend whom I played with a lot and we used to put on circuses together, and he also played brilliant piano for his age when he was a young boy. I used to dance around the room and say that I was going to be a great ballerina and he was going to be a great composer, or that he was going to be a great writer and I was going to illustrate his books. My first experience with music was at this boy's house, because he played the piano and they had old instruments like autoharps lying around. It was playing his piano that made me want to have one of my own to mess with, but then, as soon as I expressed interest, they gave me lessons and that killed it completely."

Even at seven, Joni rebelled against the constricting format of the lessons; even then she believed—although she was too young to articulate it—that creativity should flow freely and unhampered, without formalization or restriction.

At ten, Joni suffered a bout of polio, and was forced to be out of school for a year. But her mother, a qualified teacher, stayed home and gave her daughter her complete attention, keeping Joni abreast of her studies, so that the year would not be lost. In the long run, the experience was probably good for both of them, since it drew them closer together.

She first became interested in writing in the seventh grade, at Queen Elizabeth School. Looking back, she gives the credit to her teacher, Mr. Kratzman. "He encouraged us to write in any form we liked. Even at that age I enjoyed poetry, the structure of it, the dance of it, more than essays or any other form. He'd just tell us to write something. He encouraged us to love words by not criticizing our spelling or grammar, by stressing originality." Joni Mitchell's first album, *Song to a Seagull*, carries this dedication: "This album is dedicated to Mr. Kratzman, who taught me to love words."

"Later on, in the tenth grade," continued Joni, "I joined an extracurricular writers' club. Again I wrote poetry, because there wasn't much poetry assigned in the writing class. I really haven't read too much except for assigned readings in school. Even then, I only read the quota of books on the program. I've been more of a doer, especially painting. Any free time I have, I'd rather make something."

Pressed flowers and poetry aside, Joni was a doer in the healthiest sense of the word. Fresh-faced and active, she swam and she bowled, even copping trophies for her bowling. She provided artistic decorations for dances and school plays and she idolized James Dean. She drew and she painted and she sketched and, next to art, she loved dancing best. "I guess I liked the Hit Parade in those days 'cause I was looking at it from the view: can you dance to it? There wasn't much to the lyrics, although 'Get out in the kitchen and rattle those pots and pans'—that's great music, great. I love 'Shake, Rattle and Roll,' the Coasters, Chuck Berry. I've been with rock and roll

"AND HER SUNNY LOCKS HANG ON HER TEMPLES LIKE A GOLDEN FLEECE." JOAN ANDERSON, XII GRADE

from the beginning, and it's just starting to come out now."

Like most red-blooded North American kids, she was a little of what her mother considered wild. Years later, in "Let the Wind Carry Me," on her album *For the Roses* (Asylum 5057), Joni slyly hinted at her teenage rebellion:

> Mama taught me the deeper meaning
> She don't like my kick pleat skirt
> She don't like my eyelids painted green
> She don't like me staying up late
> Living for that Rock 'n' Roll dancing scene *

In her senior year in high school, Joni bought a ukelele, maybe one of the two or three most significant acts of her life, and taught herself to play it. Being able to accompany her own voice—even if it was no more than plink-plink-plunk—focused her interest onto music with a new intensity. Yet her first love remained, for the moment at least, art, and she decided to become a professional commercial artist.

"My childhood longing," she admitted to Malka, "mostly was to be a painter, yet before I went to art college my mother said to me that my stick-to-it-iveness in certain things was never that great, and she said you're going to get to art college and you're

going to get distracted, you know. Yet all I wanted to do was paint. When I got there, however, it seemed that a lot of the courses were meaningless to me and not particularly creative. And so, at the end of the year I said to my mother: 'I'm going to Toronto to become a folksinger.' And I fulfilled her prophecy. I went out and I struggled for a while."

Joni had been hanging out in Saskatoon at a coffeehouse called the Louis Riel, named after a Saskatchewan folk hero who led an insurrection against the incumbent government in the late 1800s. Strumming on her uke and singing, the golden-haired youngster earned a few dollars, which she spent on pens and ink and brushes, on a guitar and a Pete Seeger do-it-yourself instruction manual and record, and on a new baritone uke. Something was happening in her head, pulling her toward music with increasing force and power. She even got to sing on local TV, quite a step for a nineteen-year-old girl who knew only a handful of songs.

When she enrolled in the Alberta College of Art in Calgary, the distractions her mother predicted were already working in Joni's thoughts. Her inborn love of freedom and hatred of regimentation got in the way as usual, and she found many of her classes restricting and boring. There was a local coffeehouse called The Depression, and Joni began singing there, singing "real good for free." She soon scrapped the Pete Seeger demonstration record, determined to find her own style of guitar playing or give it up. "I didn't have the patience to copy a style that was already known."

Joni lasted only one year at art college. Music by then had become the overwhelming drive of her young life and, at the end of her freshman year, she made the journey east to the annual Mariposa Folk Festival. It was a three-day journey by Canadian Pacific Railroad, but a significant one. For, on the train, Joni Anderson wrote her first song. It was a blues number called "Day by Day," and it was timed to the rhythm of the train wheels, which Joni heard as a lonely, bluesy sound. She had intended to

---

return to Alberta after the festival but, when she created a minor stir there, the die seemed to be cast. Joni decided to stay in Toronto and become a professional folk-singer.

There was a burgeoning Canadian folkie scene in the mid-1960s, and Toronto's Yorkville section was the heart of it. According to Larry LeBlanc, writing in *Rolling Stone*: "Walk down the street, during an evening then, and you'd hear David Clayton-Thomas, Bonnie Dobson, Jack London and the Sparrows (later Steppenwolf), Gordon Lightfoot, the Dirty Shames, the Stormy Clovers, Elyse Weinberg, or Adam Mitchell (who joined the Paupers). Buffy Sainte-Marie wrote 'The Universal Soldier' in Yorkville. Phil Ochs wrote 'Changes' there."

Lively as the scene was, it wasn't all that easy for Joni to become a part of it. When she applied for a singing job at the River-boat, a small folk club, the club's owner, Bernie Fiedler, told her there was a job open only for a dishwasher. (Later she did sing there and she and Fiedler remain friends to this day.) Also, it cost $140 to join the musicians' union, and a union membership was necessary in order to perform. Joni worked as a salesgirl to earn the fee, then made the rounds of the clubs and coffeehouses. But most impor-tantly, she was writing, always writing — sometimes as many as four songs a week. It was almost as though, now that she knew where her heart was leading her, the music was pouring out of it.

When she did become an active part of the coffeehouse scene in Toronto, Joni kept on writing. "I was twenty, and I met kids of fifteen," she recalled later. "The things they knew, the things they were doing. My God, I blew my mind!"

Joni was playing and singing in the base-ment section of a club called the Penny Farthing in Yorkville Village when an American folksinger, Chuck Mitchell, came to the club to play the upstairs section. They met and changed the course of each other's lives. She was a tall girl, barely into her twenties, glowing with life and health, bursting with an enthusiasm for living and a volcanic talent. He was seven years older than she, a serious man and a professional

musician. In June 1965, they married; Joni Anderson had become Joni Mitchell.

Chuck Mitchell's home was in Detroit, and to Detroit the two of them went, settling down in an apartment near the campus of Wayne State University. Imme-diately they plunged into the folk music circuit, performing together as a duo. They sang a few Gordon Lightfoot songs together, Joni sang a couple of her own songs, and Chuck sang "of wars and wine," heavier material than Joni's, with a high intellectual content. Together they played clubs on the Toronto-New York-Philadelphia-Detroit circuit, including the Gaslight in New York's Greenwich Village. They began to attract attention and a following, especially Joni with her original material.

At home in Detroit, their circle of friends included folksingers better known than themselves, people like Buffy Sainte-Marie, Gordon Lightfoot, Ramblin' Jack Elliott. The Mitchells' place was frequently the scene for hilarious all-night poker games. Things began to get better professionally, especially for Joni. The Riverboat in Tor-onto booked her—and not as a dishwasher. Engagements at other folk cabarets became easier to get. She composed the title theme for a Canadian Broadcasting Corporation program, *The Way It Is*. And other singers were discovering Joni Mitchell's songs.

One night in 1966, Joni was asked to do a guest set in the Checkmate, a Detroit folk music club where the featured act was famous folksinger Tom Rush. The owner asked Rush to listen to this Canadian girl and her astonishingly original and contem-porary material.

"It was the first time I'd heard music of that genre," Tom Rush recalled in 1973. "In other words, a person who had adapted the folk idiom, writing their own material but not trying to do a folk cop, not trying to write Child Ballads, but writing their own poetry and treating it in a folky kind of way. I really loved her imagery, I think is what basically it came down to. It really got to me. Everything she said was something I could relate to, and she said it so vividly."

Rush was so knocked out by Joni and her music that he asked to include her song "Urge for Going" in his performing reper-

tory. Later he would record it on his LP *The Circle Game*, along with the title song and "Tin Angel."

But, as Joni's professional star began to shine more brightly, her marriage to Chuck Mitchell began to fall apart. Joni felt a strong need for more independence, and she began to demand it. She wanted to make it on her own, not as part of a duo, even though she retained her romanticism.

Years later, Joni gave some revealing views on marriage in an interview printed in *Maclean's*, a Canadian magazine. "I've only had one experience with it, in the legal sense of the word. But there's a kind of marriage that occurs which is almost more natural through a bonding together; sometimes the piece of paper kills something. I've talked to so many people who said, 'Our relationship was beautiful until we got married.' If I ever married again I would like to create a ceremony and a ritual that had more meaning than I feel our present-day ceremonies have. Just a declaration to a group of friends. If two people are in love and they declare to a room of people that they are in love—somehow or other, that's almost like a marriage vow. It tells everybody in the room: 'I'm no longer flirting with you. I'm no longer available because I've declared my heart to this person.'"

"She always had a strong visceral sense of what to do," Chuck told *Time* magazine with some bitterness. "She knew she was beginning to happen and needed out. She was into her Magic Princess trip. Her first hits were for people who were frustrated, unhappy, and also living in a fantasy world."

Not much more than a year after they were married, Joni Mitchell left her husband and headed east. Her destination was the Mecca of all folksingers, New York's Greenwich Village and its star-studded folk music haunts, like the Limelight, the Cafe au Go Go, and, most of all, Gerde's Folk City, where Bob Dylan got his start.

Folk music had undergone some heavy changes in the last twenty-five years. In the late 1930s and throughout the 1940s, there were three mainstreams of "folk" music, each very different from the other two. First, there was the classic, purist music, originally from Britain, sometimes called Child Ballads after the American philologist who collected them. These were recorded by Alan Lomax in the southern Appalachian mountains, and sung by such artists as Susan Reed, a beautiful redhead who plucked a dulcimer and other archaic stringed instruments. Richard Dyer-Bennett, a pure-voiced tenor, was another exponent of the Child-type ballad. Dressed in white tie and tails, he would sit on the stage of Carnegie Hall, throw back his aristocratic blond head, and from his high-arched, bony nose would issue laments for virgins slain by jealous sisters, knights who died for unrequited love, and endless choruses of "Waly Waly." "Greensleeves" was the big popular number among the Child Ballad cognoscenti, followed closely by "The Golden Vanity."

The second stream, masculine and vital, was the itinerant worker music of the Depression thirties. Technically, this was not "folk" music at all, because the songs were not anonymous, but written by such men as Woody Guthrie, Pete Seeger, and Lee Hayes. Guthrie's Dust Bowl Ballads were the protest songs of his generation, chronicling the tribulations of farmers turned away by banks from the barren land to wander homeless, the new class of America's poor. Guthrie's was music with balls, and it had a far-reaching effect on the liberal consciousness of middle-class white America. In New York, Jewish kids whose parents would have fits if they came home after 10 p.m. were bellowing out lyrics about having no home and just a-wanderin' round, and labor-minded youngsters who could not even imagine the *outside* of a mine were caroling knowledgeably about events in Harlan County, where you either are a union man or a stooge for J. H. Blair (whoever he was). This was left-wing music, but these were left-wing times. Guthrie's influence reached even as remote a place as Hibbings, Minnesota, where a curly-haired young man named Robert Zimmerman paid it strict attention.

The third stream of folk music flowed deeply black, and was fed by twin underground rivers—work songs and blues. Sonny

Terry and Brownie McGhee, Lightnin' Hopkins, and Big Bill Broonzy, among others, carried this music from the black people to those white people who would listen, and Josh White actually brought it into the chic cafes and supper clubs, singing "John Henry" in no less a place than New York's Blue Angel, a sophisticated night club. But the giant of this music was a convicted pimp and murderer whose songs of prison life—"Midnight Special," "Goodnight Irene," and others—were bellowed out lustily by boys and girls who never had and never would lay eyes on Huddie Ledbetter. Old "Leadbelly" and his twelve-string guitar were the essence of the depressed black experience; this was a man who had paid heavy dues to sing and write the blues.

This then was the essence of the folk scene up to around 1950—Olde Englishe, Guthrie-Wobbly, and black blues. There were few folk groups of any merit—most of the acts were singles. Tom Paley led a little band of singers called the American Folksay Group, which would later meld quietly into the New Lost City Ramblers. Oscar Brand had a radio program over a city-sponsored noncommercial New York City station; it was possible to schlep down to WNYC on a Sunday morning and sit nose-to-nose with Josh White, Pete Seeger, or Jean Ritchie. It was impossible to attend a Henry Wallace-for-President rally or an American Youth for Democracy meeting without folksingers being present also. If you danced Friday nights at Ethical Culture, there was a good chance that Leadbelly himself would drop in during the break, and you'd all sit on the floor and join in the chorus: "Let the midnight SPESHHH-ull shine its ever-lovin' light on meeeeeee."

It would be another decade before Bob Dylan would unite all three streams into an overflowing river of contemporary music, but in 1950 something significant happened: The Weavers. A pickin' and singin', ebullient group that included the ubiquitous Pete Seeger, as well as Lee Hayes and pert Ronnie Gilbert, the Weavers broke into the Top Forty with, of all things, Leadbelly's "Goodnight, Irene." The entire nation, tuned into AM radio, was clapping hands to

"Irene" and "On Top of Old Smokey." Folk music had come out.

The first Newport Folk Festival was held in 1959, and included were not only the performers who had been on the scene for years, but also a representation from the three musical tributaries of Appalachian mountain ballads, workingman songs, and black blues. Among those singing there were Pete Seeger, Sonny Terry and Brownie McGhee, Jean Ritchie and John Jacob Niles, Leon Bibb and Earl Scruggs.

Also in 1959, the smashing success of the Kingston Trio—with "Tom Dooley" number one on the charts—inspired impresario Albert Grossman to create the perfect folk trio to match—Peter, Paul and Mary—and thus the door was opened to Joan Baez and Bob Dylan, to Judy Collins, Theodore Bikel, Odetta, Tom Rush, and Buffy Sainte-Marie, and, later, to Joni Mitchell.

Coffeehouses and folk music clubs sprang up all over—Chicago's Gate of Horn, the Golden Vanity in Boston, Club 47 in Cambridge where Joan Baez began. And Gerde's Folk City in New York's Greenwich Village, which was the folk equivalent of playing the Palace. And there were folk festivals from Newport to Miami Beach to Mariposa in Toronto.

Beginning in 1965 when Dylan, to the hisses and boos of the purists, went electric, the folk scene started to wane. By the end of that year, folk had gone from folk-protest to folk-rock, which was also heavily into protest. Joni, who was neither wired for amplification nor wired into political protest, had no ambitions, she claimed later, of becoming a superstar like Baez or Dylan. Her goals were shorter-term, more modest.

"I always kept my goals very short. Like I would like to play in a coffeehouse, so I did. I would like to play in the United States, you know, the States, the magic of crossing the border. So I did. I would like to make a certain amount of money a year, which I thought would give me the freedom to buy the clothes that I wanted and the antiques and just some women trips, a nice apartment in New York that I wouldn't have to be working continually to support. But I had no idea that I would be this successful, especially since I came to folk music when it was already dying.

"The year Dylan went electric, the folk clubs started closing all over the country. It was an epidemic. The only people being hired were people who had records out. I was always bringing up the rear. In those days, if you only played acoustical guitar, club owners treated you as though you were a dinosaur. Now everyone's branching out," said Joni in a 1969 interview, "and there's room for all styles. People are playing where they feel their music."

Soon after coming to New York, she settled into a little one-bedroom apartment between Fifth and Sixth Avenues on Sixteenth Street, and began building her fantasy castles for her "Magic Princess trip." *Time* magazine reported that "she covered one bedroom wall in tinfoil, festooned the doorjambs with crepe paper. She toyed with writing a children's book about mythical kingdoms and later celebrated her new freedom in 'Chelsea Morning.'"

A lot of long-haired, blue jean ladies were into the bells, beads, and tinfoil trip then. But only a Joni Mitchell could distill the experience into "Chelsea Morning."

Her little apartment, with its brick wall and its fireplace, faced the street. The district, just north of Greenwich Village, is charming and old-fashioned, just the sort of neighborhood to appeal to Joni; it is called Chelsea. And even in sooty, polluted New York, the sun does sometimes "pour in like butterscotch." It was not only "Chelsea Morning" that Joni wrote in this apartment, but "Michael from Mountains" as well.

By now, Joni was becoming known to singers of some fame because of her original songs. Like Laura Nyro and later, Carole King, she was destined to hear her music recorded and interpreted by others before she would have the chance to do it herself. Tom Rush had recorded "Tin Angel," "The Circle Game," and "Urge for Going." Buffy Sainte-Marie had recorded "The Circle Game" and "Ode to a Seagull." And her most celebrated interpreter, Judy Collins, who would one day sell a million copies of "Both Sides Now," had discovered Joni's music too. But that was the inside world, the world of her colleagues. The outside world had yet to know her name, but that was just about to change.

PHOTOGRAPHER UNKNOWN. NEWPORT FOLK FESTIVAL, 1968, WITH GRAHAM NASH

In the fall of 1967, Joni was doing a fifteen-dollar-a-night gig at the Cafe au Go Go in the Village, singing as the opening act for Richie Havens. A hot young agent-manager named Elliot Roberts was persuaded by one of his clients, Buffy Sainte-Marie, to go and hear Joni Mitchell, a dynamite young songwriter. Roberts was stunned by the talent of this blue-eyed farm girl with the flowing blonde hair.

"I just saw her and went back after the

Today, Elliot Roberts is a superstar among artists' managers, with a prestigious stable of entertainers. His roster reads like a musical *Who's Who*.

David Crosby, of Crosby, Stills, Nash, and Young, who was among those rock stars managed by Roberts, described him thus to *Rolling Stone*:

"Elliot Roberts is a good dude. And he is not a fair-weather friend, and he is not a bullshitter. However, he is, in his managerial

DAVID GAHR. 1969

show and she blew my mind," said Roberts. "She had all those songs then and I just went back and told her I wanted to manage her. I would do anything to work with her." Although Joni was, in Roberts' words, "a jumble of creative clutter, with a guitar case full of napkins, road maps, and scraps of paper all covered with lyrics," Roberts didn't hesitate. Cutting his ties with his management company, he gave up all his other clients to devote his entire energies to Joni Mitchell.

capacity, capable of lying straight-faced to anyone, anytime, ever. But he's really a beautiful cat, he really has a heart and it's plain that he does. You just naturally do get to love the cat . . . unless you gotta write a contract with him. In which case you may just never want to speak to him again, 'cause he not only doesn't give away anything, he's armed robbery in a business deal.

"And if he doesn't rob you blind he'll send David Geffen [then with CMA] over;

he'll take your whole company. And sell it while you're out to lunch. Those two guys, man, are not kidding. And they understand what's going on. Don't think it's any mistake that Elliot Roberts could step into the managing of artists business and in two years be holding a couple of million dollars' worth of stuff. I mean, he didn't do it by being stupid, right? And he didn't do it by just picking the right people. He made good moves. I could name a dozen. Y'know, he's really bright at it, but he's really a human being. A rarity."

Elliot Roberts put the finishing, smoothing touches to Joni's act. Andy Wickham signed her to a Reprise recording contract. Then, Roberts made another of his brilliant moves. He pried Joni out of New York and took her to Los Angeles. Now her business interests were being looked after by professionals.

L.A.—the City of the Angels—was a vital, flourishing center of contemporary sounds when Joni arrived there in 1968. The focus of power had shifted from the heavy, psychedelic funk music of San Francisco; now a prettier, softer and more melodic sound was emerging—as personified by the Mamas and the Papas, the Beach Boys, the Byrds. It was, of course, the perfect place for Joni, although she was wary of L.A. at first. She found it a strange, bad-vibes kind of city, dominated by automobiles. Joni had become accustomed to wandering anonymously through the streets of New York, seeking inspirations for her story-songs, talking to New York characters and crazies, wise men and winos. "In a pure anonymous encounter you find a world alive and full of character," she said. "In New York, the street adventures are incredible. There are a thousand stories in a single block. You see the stories in people's faces. You hear the songs immediately. Here, in Los Angeles, there are fewer characters because they're all inside automobiles. You don't see them on park benches or peeing in the gutter or any of that."

Joni laid down the tracks for her first album, *Song to a Seagull* (Reprise 6293), and made an appearance at the most prestigious folk club in Los Angeles, the Troubadour. She still hated the city. "I was raised in a country town in Saskatchewan, and I thought that the city was a glamorous, glittering place. But I discovered that it is vulgar, plastic, in a rush for a dollar." Yet, a kind of love began to grow for Los Angeles—the same love-hate relationship Joni had felt for New York and expressed on her first album—and eventually she could honestly write the lyrics, "I'm your biggest fan, California," and, in "Court and

JOSEPH SIA. ATLANTIC CITY POP FESTIVAL, 1969

Spark": "But I couldn't let go of L.A., city of the fallen angels." California is a recurrent theme in Joni's albums; she still lives there a large part of the year, in a house in Bel Air.

With the release of *Song to a Seagull*, Joni reached out to a much wider audience, and became an important fixture of the contemporary music scene. 1969 was a busy and productive year for Joni, bringing increasing rewards. She played the Miami Pop Festival, where she scored a big hit. The year before, the manager of the Festival,

Tom Rounds, had publicly doubted her pulling power over that of Creedence Clearwater Revival, a top rock group. "Why overshadow a talent like Joni Mitchell with a Creedence Clearwater Revival?" he'd asked. "If you do book both to appear on the same day, the audience merely tolerates Joni Mitchell and everyone else, waiting for the superstars." The day when an audience would "merely tolerate" Joni was over almost before it began; she was to prove herself a top attraction before the year was out.

Joni sang at the Newport Folk Festival that year, too, making an impression on the audience that was not easy to eradicate. Jim Marshall and Baron Wolman, authors of *Festival*! (Macmillan, Collier Books), recall her: "Joni Mitchell pursing her lips, eyes closed, hands clasped, shoulders hunched, bent into the stand microphone, one moment looking like a young widow, the next, when she breaks the anguished stance and runs her voice up an octave or two, looking like a woman seeing her lover come into view after an absence of a month."

In July of 1969, Joni shared a stage with Tim Hardin at New York's Schaefer Music Festival. Dressed in a long sea-green gown that brought out the color of her long flowing hair, she sang songs about the city while accompanying herself on guitar, piano, and dulcimer.

She also did a national tour as the open-

ing act for Crosby, Stills, and Nash, then the hottest band in the country. She traveled a great deal in 1969.

"I just played in Saskatoon, my home town," she told *Time* magazine, "and it was a tremendously emotional experience. When I sang 'Both Sides Now,' it was like singing the words for the first time."

Joni bought a house in Laurel Canyon, and moved into it with Graham Nash, an Englishman who had formerly been with the Hollies, and who had just joined up with David Crosby and Stephen Stills to form Crosby, Stills, and Nash. About three miles north of the "Strip," as Hollywood's Sunset Strip is familiarly known, Laurel Canyon is a hilly, tree-filled canyon that

tiques and pussycats and her favorite possessions. "It's a great place," she enthused to reporter Sandra Shevey, "with stained-glass windows, oak beam wooden floors, a Priestly piano and a grandfather clock. [The clock was the gift of singer-poet and fellow-Canadian Leonard Cohen.] Both Tom Mix and Houdini have lived there. I've always been fascinated by supernatural power," Joni confided. "When I was a little girl I tried for weeks to change candle wax into jewels after I saw an alchemist do it in *Tales of Hoffman.*"

Happy and open, Graham and Joni entertained both friends and reporters there, in the pine-paneled house at the foot of the hills. "It's a lovely house," wrote the

HENRY DILTZ   NEXT PAGE: JIM MARSHALL

is one of Los Angeles's hippest addresses, especially among the younger members of the music world. When Joni and Graham lived together, their near neighbors were Stills, Crosby, and Cass Elliot of the Mamas and the Papas.

The house, a two-bedroom affair that made up for in homey charm what it lacked in elegance, was stuffed by Joni with an-

august New York *Times* in April of 1969, "sunny and friendly and filled with the easy-going good spirits of the Laurel Canyon music scene. There's a lot going on there; Joni is in the midst of recording her second album and Nash is doing the album with Crosby and Stills."

The media all but knocked one another over in their race to catalog the possessions

that cluttered the house, and none of them left out either Joni's special favorite of the two cats, Hunter, a nine-year-old tom, or Joni's favorite cat of all—Graham Nash. ("Our house," Graham would write and sing later, "is a very, very, very fine house, with two cats in the yard. . . .") ". . . two cats, a stuffed elk head," listed the New York *Times*, "a grandfather clock given her by Leonard Cohen, a king's head with a jeweled crown sticking out from the brick fireplace, votive candles, blooming azaleas, a turkey made of pinecones, dried flowers, old dolls, Victorian shadow boxes, colored glass, an ornamental plate from Saskatoon, an art nouveau lamp in the shape of a frog holding a lily pad, a collection of cloisonné boxes, bowls and ashtrays, patchwork quilts, Maxfield Parrish pictures, various musical instruments, and Graham Nash."

"Antique pieces crowd the tables, mantels and shelves," *Rolling Stone* confided to its readers. "There are antique handbags hung on a bathroom wall, a hand-carved hat rack at the door; there are castle-style doors and Tiffany stained-glass windows. Nash is perched on an English church chair, and Joni is in the kitchen, using the only electric lights on in the house. She's making the crust for a rhubarb pie."

Time was rather less kind to Joni's precious possessions, in the usual manner of *Time*'s celebrated snideness. In 1969, they wrote: "She lives in a ramshackle house in Los Angeles's Laurel Canyon, with second-hand trappings." On *Time*'s list: ". . . brown velvet rockers, black and yellow crocheted throws, a giant antique wooden pig, an old piano, a doll [there were actually several], stained-glass windowpanes, and a sewing machine on which she makes her own dresses."

It is difficult to overemphasize the importance of the Laurel Canyon house or Joni's relationship with Graham Nash—or "Willy," as everybody called him. For a while it was a haven of peace and love, and, most especially, of music. Also, it fulfilled the basic nesting needs and domestic urges that lay deep in Joni's nature, one of the three strong conflicting sides to her personality. When Joni described Trina, Annie, and Estrella, Laurel Canyon ladies all, in her song "Ladies of the Canyon,"

she was—consciously or unconsciously—describing herself.

"Trina wears her wampum beads and fills her drawing book with line"—that's Joni Mitchell. "Annie sits you down to eat. She always makes you welcome in"—that's Joni Mitchell. "Estrella circus girl comes wrapped in songs and gypsy shawls"—and *that's* Joni as well. Even if she meant Estrella to be Mama Cass, and Annie and Trina to be other ladies, the descriptions fit Joni herself perfectly. Trina weaving a pattern with her paints and threads, Annie baking breads and gathering flowers for her home, and Estrella pouring music down the canyon, coloring the sunhine hours—who could deny their resemblance to their creator?

The Laurel Canyon house was a focus for a great deal of musical activity. David Crosby described some of it later. "One night we were at Joni Mitchell's. Ah, there's a story! Cass was there. Stephen was there, me and Willy (Graham Nash), just us five hangin' out. You know how it is this night, I mean this time of night, so we were singin', as you would imagine. What happened was we started singin' a country song of Stephen's called 'Helplessly Hoping.' And I had already worked out the third harmony. Stephen and I started singin' it, Willy looked at the rafters for about ten seconds, listened, and started singin' the other part like he'd been singin' it all his life. That's how Willy does things. And the feeling of that, man, was like havin' somebody give you head all of a sudden in a sound sleep. It was like waking up on acid. I couldn't begin to tell you how that was. That was a heavy flash, 'cause that's a nice thing. You know it was. Especially if you're a harmony singer and you love singin' harmony. And I am and I do and it got me off. So that's what we were doing."

"But isn't there a certain amount of danger," Joni was asked later, "when you surround yourself with musicians and troubadours doing the same kind of work you are doing, that you really create your own special world and are not so open to what's happening in the rest of the world?"

"A friend of mine," replied Joni, "criticized me for that. He said that my work was becoming very 'inside.' It was making reference to roadies and rock 'n' rollers, and

JIM MARSHALL. MONTEREY FOLK FESTIVAL, 1969, WITH STEPHEN STILLS

NEXT PAGE: JIM MARSHALL. MONTEREY FOLK FESTIVAL, 1969, WITH JOHN SEBASTIAN, STEPHEN STILLS, GRAHAM NASH, AND DAVID CROSBY

that's the very thing I didn't want to happen, why I like to take a lot of time off to travel some place where I can have my anonymity and I can have that day-to-day encounter with other walks of life. But it gets more and more difficult.

"That's the wonderful thing about being a successful playwright or an author, you still maintain your anonymity, which is very important in order to be somewhat of a voyeur, to collect your observations for your material. And to suddenly often be the center of attention—it threatened the writer in me. The performer threatened the writer."

Her privacy has always been of paramount importance to Joni. She confided to Sandra Shevey, in an interview for her book, *The Ladies of Pop-Rock*, "I've always been plagued by a fear of success: that it would be a fishbowl. When I was fourteen I remember sitting in the beauty parlor having my hair set for the Senior Prom. I was reading a fan magazine about Sandra Dee and Bobby Darin and I thought: How awful it would be to have your life in headlines. Now I can't walk through a crowd anymore and forget who I am."

With the release of Joni's second album,

Clouds (Reprise 6341), which had an advance sale of 100,000 copies a month before release, things began to darken in her private life. For one thing, the autobiographical nature of her lyrics made it possible to speculate on just "who" it was the songs were written for. "Lately," she complained in 1969, "life has been constantly filled with interruptions. I don't have five hours in a row to myself. I think I'm less prolific now, but I'm also more demanding of myself. I have many melodies in my mind at all times, but the words are different now. It's mainly because I rely on my own experiences for lyrics."

Growing fame (Joni won a Grammy Award in 1969 for *Clouds*: Best Folk Performance) made it almost impossible to hold onto any privacy or to move around with any sense of freedom. Although she hadn't been at Woodstock, her song "Woodstock," recorded by Crosby, Stills, Nash, and Neil Young, had made her a superstar. "Woodstock" was defined again and again as the anthem of the flower-child generation. But Joni's love relationship with Graham Nash had broken up, and Joni withdrew herself from her devoted audiences and from media speculation over her famous lovers. She

ROBERT ALTMAN, MONTEREY, 1969

ROBERT ALTMAN. MONTEREY, 1969

and Warren Beatty. Joni decided to split.

"I have in my time been very misunderstood," she told a journalist. "All people seemed interested in was the music and the gossip. I felt then that the music spoke for itself and the gossip was unimportant."

Her lovers were obviously a sensitive subject to Joni; why should her work be defined by its superficial rather than its deeper meaning? Also, it was obvious that here was no ordinary, run-of-the-mill "old lady"; why should she be restricted to one relationship and why should that relationship be with an ordinary person? Why should her relationships be endlessly dissected and snickered over? Like gravitates to like; Joni, high-energy superstar, met and was attracted by—and also was attractive to —other high-energy superstars of creativity, men with the same drives that she had. Graham Nash said of her, "When you fall for Joan, you fall all the way. She means a lot to a great number of people."

Yet, it would be years before she could discuss her lovers in print, and then only with an old friend, folksinger Malka. "Your name has been linked to some powerful people in the business," stated the interviewer. "James Taylor and Graham Nash,

was bored and disgusted with hearing endless guesses about Stills and Nash, about Leonard Cohen, Neil Young, James Taylor,

JIM MARSHALL. MONTEREY, 1969

for instance. Do you feel that your friends have helped your career in any way?"

Joni shook her head. "I don't think so, not in the time that James and I were spending together, anyway. He was a total unknown, for one thing—maybe I helped his career?

"But I do think that when creative people come together, the stimulus of the relationship is bound to show. The rock and roll industry is very incestuous, you know. We have all interacted and we have all been the source of many songs for one another. We have all been close at one time or another, and I think that a lot of beautiful music came from it. A lot of beautiful times came from it, too, through that mutual understanding. A lot of pain, too, because, inevitably, different relationships broke up.

"I hang my laundry on the line when I write. People make judgments and it's none of their business. It almost makes me decide not to write anything but fiction, but I have to do my thing."

She made an unsuccessful attempt at psychoanalysis, hoping to ease her depression and discover who she really was and how she could resolve the paradoxical sides of her nature to bring her both the freedom of artistic expression and the comfort of a successful love that she so desperately wanted.

"A couple of years ago I got very, very depressed, to the point where I thought it was no longer a problem to burden my friends with. I was practically catatonic." The psychiatrist she consulted asked her if she ever felt suicidal. When Joni told him that she had never considered suicide as an option, "he handed me his card and said, 'Listen. Call me again sometime when you feel suicidal.' And I went out into the street. So many priests and psychiatrists miss the whole point of getting right to the heart of a person."

Joni had been spending up to forty weeks a year on the road, communicating her sincerity to her fans, laying out her private life

JIM MARSHALL. MONTEREY, 1969, WITH MIMI FARINA

HENRY DILTZ. LAUREL CANYON

in her songs. Now, sick of everybody's probing, she announced a sort of retirement, and canceled two major public appearances, Carnegie Hall in New York and Constitution Hall in Washington, D.C.

"In January [1970] I did my last concert. I played in London and I came home. In February I finished up my record. I gave my last concert with the idea that I'd take this year off, because I need new material. I need new things to say in order to perform, so there's something in it for me. You can't just sing the same songs."

Later, she told a British reporter: "When I retired I felt I never really wanted to play in front of people again—ever. I'd gained a strange perspective on performing. I had a bad attitude about it, you know. I felt like what I was writing was too personal to be applauded for. I even thought that maybe the thing to do was to present the song some different way—like a play or a classical performance where you play everything and then run off stage and let them do whatever they want, applaud or walk out.

"After a while, when people come up and say they love a song it begins to sound hollow and you meet so many people that misunderstood what you said. It is appreciated when someone says it and genuinely means it, and you can see it's moved them, maybe changed them a little. Like I've really been moved by some performances and I've been unable to tell them from my side of it, because I know what it's like to receive praise. It's a very difficult thing to give sincerely and communicate that sincerity."

When Joni retired, her manager, Elliot Roberts, explained it this way: "She performs in cycles when she feels that she has a lot of fresh material that she enjoys playing and therefore wants to bring to the public. She doesn't like to work when she feels she's just been repetitious, so when she writes another five, six or seven songs she'll probably want to play them for the public again, and then she'll go back to work. That's why she works basically every two years, because then she has six or seven new songs she's proud of."

But there was more to Joni's announced retreat than a downward arc of the cycle. A great insecurity, a powerful feeling of loneliness and confusion was threatening to envelop her. "You ask yourself a lot of questions," she stated. "You tailor-make your dreams to 'it'll be this way' and when it isn't . . . I was too close to my own work."

Joni was finding other aspects of success difficult to deal with as well. One of them was money. "I had difficulty at one point accepting my affluence," she told Malka, "and my success and even the expression of it seemed to me distasteful at one time. Like to be suddenly driving a fancy car. I had a lot of soul-searching to do as I felt somehow or other that living in elegance and luxury canceled creativity. I still had the stereotyped idea that success would deter creativity, would stop the gift, that luxury would make you too comfortable and complacent and that the gift would suffer from it.

"But I found the only way that I could reconcile with myself and my art was to say: this is what I'm going through now, my life is changing and I am, too. I'm an extremist as far as lifestyle goes. I need to live simply and primitively sometimes, at least for short periods of the year, in order to keep in touch with something more basic.

"But I have come to be able to finally enjoy my success and to use it as a form of self-expression, and not to deny it. Leonard Cohen has a line that says, 'Do not dress in these rags for me. I know you are not poor.' And when I heard that line I thought to myself that I had been denying, which was a sort of a hypocritical thing. I began to feel too separate from my audience and from my times. I wanted to hitchhike and scuffle. I felt maybe I hadn't done enough scuffling."

Joni told Larry LeBlanc, "I was being isolated, starting to feel like a bird in a gilded cage. I wasn't getting a chance to meet people. A certain amount of success cuts you off in a lot of ways. You can't move

PHILIP GOTLOP/CAMERA PRESS, LONDON

KARL FERRIS, IBIZA, 1970

freely. I like to live, be on the streets, to be in a crowd and moving freely." She remembered the anonymous encounters with the characters of New York, and the faces and stories that helped inspire her early songs.

Confusion, depression and a lack of freedom all combined to make it urgently apparent to Joni that she must find something or someone to turn to for help.

Where do you turn when you've nobody to turn to? Joni decided to take a prolonged vacation, to travel around the globe in search of herself. On a trip to Hawaii, she was horrified by the highways and the asphalt, the pollution and the concrete defacing the magnificent tropical landscape of that state. "Big Yellow Taxi" was written in a burst of wry outrage, and it soon became a staple song in her repertoire. Bob Dylan recorded it, too. And Joni kept on traveling. "I wanted more than a release. I wanted some wisdom, some kind of counsel and direction." She traveled on, looking to get herself into focus and find inner peace.

In the summer of 1970, she took a break from her self-imposed exile and went to sing

KARL FERRIS. IBIZA, LISTENING TO TAJ MAHAL

KARL FERRIS. IBIZA, 1970

38

at the Mariposa Folk Festival, in Toronto. It was more of a hometown reunion for her than a public appearance, because Mariposa and Toronto were where she'd got her real first start. More relaxed than she'd been, making her first public appearance in more than six months, she gave a long interview to *Rolling Stone*'s Larry LeBlanc, in which she talked about her travels.

"I've been to Greece, Spain, France, and from Jamaica to Panama, through the Canal. Some of my friends were moving their boat from Fort Lauderdale up to San Francisco. I joined them in Jamaica and sailed down through the Canal. It was really an experience."

Perhaps the highlight of her travels was a long visit to Crete. "To me, it was a lovely life, far better than being middle class in America. I lived for five weeks in a cave there. The only trouble was it was very commercialized. The magazines were writing it up. As a result, you had a lot of prying tourists all of the time. Even that was kinda funny, because most of the people living in the caves were Canadians, Americans, Swiss, and French. They'd say, 'Oh, here come the tourists.' It was kind of funny, the Greeks being the tourists."

Joni went on to describe the caves as being "on high sedimentary cliffs, sandstone, a lot of seashells in it. The caves were carved out by the Minoans hundreds of years ago [she probably meant thousands of years; Minoan civilization was destroyed forever about five thousand years ago]. Then they were used later on for leper caves. Then after that the Romans came, and they used them for burial crypts. Then some of them were filled in and sealed up for a long time. People began living there, beatniks, in the fifties. Kids gradually dug out more rooms. There were some people there who were wearing human teeth necklaces around their necks."

Living in a cave in Crete was an unusual experience and a very pleasant one. "We all put on a lot of weight," Joni told *Rolling Stone*. "We were eating a lot of apple pies, good bacon. We were eating really well, good wholesome food. The village pretty well survived on the tourist trade, which was the kids who lived in the caves. I don't know what their business was before people came. There were a couple of fishing boats that went out, that got enough fish to supply the two restaurants there.

"The bakery lady who had the grocery store there had fresh bread, fresh rice pudding, made nice yogurt every day, and did a thriving business. Just before I left she installed a refrigerator. She had the only cold drinks in town. It was all chrome and glass. It was a symbol of her success.

"Then the cops came and kicked everyone out of the caves, but it was getting a little crazy there. Everybody was getting a little crazy there. Everybody was getting more and more into open nudity. They were really going back to the caveman. They were wearing little loincloths. The Greeks couldn't understand what was happening."

Truly a description of the ultimate hippie experience, one that left Joni missing her "clean white linen and expensive French cologne." So she moved on, back to Paris and civilization.

Meanwhile, *Melody Maker*, Great Britain's most important music magazine, voted Joni top female performer of the year; she was obviously in the forefront, whether performing or not.

And Joni, traveling or at home, never stopped writing. She released *Blue* (Reprise 2038) in 1971, her most intensely personal, autobiographical, and painful album to date. Containing anguished laments for her lost love with Graham Nash, and bittersweet backward looks at her relationship with James Taylor, *Blue* found a wider audience than any of her earlier albums. She was at an incredible peak of creativity; she appeared to be made entirely of sensitivity, every nerve exposed on the album.

Freed from the Hollywood scene, Joni sold the Laurel Canyon house, remarking with wry bitterness, "It was just an address," which was somewhat unfair to the happy days (and many of them were happy) she'd spent there. In its place, Joni built a house by the sea north of Vancouver, a house built sparely of native stone and surrounded by forty acres of beloved privacy. There, she can find the time and the peace of mind to paint, write, practice her music, and commune with silence and nature. Frequently,

she walks nude to the sea. In short, she is keeping in touch with something more basic.

"The land has a rich melancholy about it," she says. "Not in summer because it's usually very clear. But in the spring and winter it's very brooding and it's conducive to a certain kind of thinking. I find if I just sit around and meditate and mope about it all then there's no release at all. I just get deeper and deeper into it. Whereas in the art of creating—when the song is born and you've made something beautiful—it's a release valve."

Joni returned to the concert stage in 1972, traveling and appearing with Jackson Browne, then comparatively unknown except for one hit, "Doctor My Eyes." Both she and Browne were nominated to *Esquire*'s annual rock roundup, the "Heavy 100." About her, the magazine said, "Somehow all other folky girl singers seem to be in eclipse. Joni doesn't work much, but her records are superior, tougher." Among the other artists chosen for the select list were Bette Midler, David Bowie, Elton John,

Labelle, Billy Preston, Marvin Gaye, the Eagles, Emerson, Lake & Palmer, Carly Simon and Paul Simon, Rod Stewart, and the Rolling Stones. But *Esquire* wasn't all good taste or fine prescience. Also on the list could be found David Cassidy, the Osmonds (and if they qualify as rock heavies, then the term "rock" needs some redefinition), John Prine, Patti Smith, Pamela Polland, Sun Ra, and Todd Rundgren.

Also in 1972, *For the Roses* was released, Joni's first album for David Geffen's label, Asylum (Asylum 0598). On the album cover, Joni appeared calm and half-smiling, dressed in boots and velvets, a princess among the pine trees. Inside the album, when you turned past a felt-marker portrait of a bunch of roses, courtesy Joni Mitchell, you came upon Joni again, roaming naked to the Pacific Ocean, standing like a naiad upon the rocks, washed by the ocean's spray. "Directed" by the team of Roberts and Geffen, *For the Roses* presented far more sophisticated musical ar-

JIM MARSHALL, LAUREL CANYON, 1971

41

rangements than Joni's listeners had come to expect.

The piano was important, as it was in *Blue*, where Joni had used it heavily. But she had added Tom Scott on woodwinds and reeds, Bobby Notkoff on strings, Graham Nash on harmonica, and others on percussion, drums, and electric guitar. And she had a hit single as well. "You Turn Me On, I'm a Radio," written (they say) for Los Angeles disc jockey B. Mitchell Reed, climbed up the charts.

Financial insecurity was not one of the problems that had been plaguing Joni Mitchell. Brilliantly managed by Elliot Roberts, she had become the owner of a music publishing corporation worth at least a million and a half dollars as early as 1969. By 1973, she owned two such corporations, as well as valuable real estate. Although not worried about money itself, she did give a generous thought to some of the best ways of putting it to use working for others.

"Then there comes the question," she said, "of do you take it all for yourself or what do you put back into the world? I haven't really found what I am to do. People are always coming up with great causes for me to get involved in and they have wonderful arguments and reasons why I should be. The ones I select are the ones that I am genuinely interested in because I feel they will show some sort of immediate return. Maybe this is impatience; like in the Greenpeace, we raised some money to buy the ship which went to Amchitka, with the hopes that they were going to sit in the territorial waters in this area where they're exploding bombs ridiculously close to the San Andreas fault. That inflamed me. That was a project I wanted to be a part of. In Montreal I played at a benefit for Cree Indians who were being displaced by a very stupidly run dam project.

"I know that money can be put to positive use, even if it's just to support people struggling in the arts. I believe in art. I believe that it's very important that people be encouraged in their self-expression and

43

that their self-expression ping-pongs someone else's self-expression. That's what I believe in the most. If I'm going to distribute some of my windfall, it would be among other artists."

And, also on the subject of money, she made up a wry little ditty for *Time* magazine:

Zsa Zsa's got her jewels
Minnie's got her chickens to go
I've got my corporations
I'm a capitalistic so and so.

Somewhat refreshed in spirit, freed of a number of her insecurities, Joni celebrated her thirtieth birthday by planning a long concert tour, a complete return to the stage. But first, *Court and Spark* (Asylum 7E-1001) was released to a delighted public. It was Joni's most popular album ever, and it contained not one but three hit songs, "Help Me," "Raised on Robbery," and "Free Man in Paris," the last-named an obvious reference to record mogul David Geffen who stokes "the starmaker machinery behind the popular song."

For the first time in her recording career, Joni recorded a song that wasn't her own original creation—"Twisted," by Ross and Grey, a jazzy upbeat song about a nut who doesn't care if her analyst does tell her she's crazy. "I love that song," Joni commented. "I always have loved it. I went through analysis for a while this year and the song is about analysis. I figured that I earned the right to sing it. I tried to put it on the last record but it was totally inappropriate. It had nothing to do with that time period and some of my friends feel that it has nothing to do with this album either. It's added like an encore."

When she was asked why she had gone through analysis at this period in her life, Joni replied, "I felt I wanted to talk to someone about confusion which we all have. I wanted to talk to someone and I was willing to pay for his discretion. I didn't expect him to have the answers or that he was a guru or anything, only a sounding board for a lot of things. And it proved effective, because simply by confronting paradoxes or difficulties within your life several times a week, they seem not to be so important as they do when they're weighing on your mind in the middle of the night, by yourself, with no one to talk to, or someone to talk to who will probably tell another friend who will just tell another friend, as friends do.

"I felt that I didn't want to burden people close to me, so I paid for professional help. And I went through a lot of changes about it, too. It's like driving out your

S. Singer. 1973, with Tom Scott and the LA Express

devils—do you drive out your angels as well? You know that whole thing about the creative process. An artist needs a certain amount of turmoil and confusion, and I've created out of that. It's been like part of the creative force—even out of the severe depression there comes insight. It's sort of masochistic to dwell on it, but you know it helps you to gain understanding.

"I think analysis did me a lot of good."

Joni's 1974 concert tour brought her to the stage for some seventy-two performances, an exhausting schedule. Backed up by Tom Scott and the L.A. Express, Joni sang jazzy and she sang rock 'n' roll, moving further than ever from the folk style she'd started out with a decade before. She appeared confident and friendly, and the two-record album that was cut from a handful of those concerts, *Miles of Aisles* (Asylum AB 202), bubbled over with exuberance and jazzy arrangements. The concerts themselves went well; in the past Joni had stood alone with her music, creating and delivering it with solo voice and instrument. Now she had her backup men in an ensemble that produced a more rocking sound and rhythmic beat. It was almost dancing music, and it revealed Joni as a mature woman—over thirty now and no longer a girl—who was on top of her life and her music. She had made the transition from folk-contemporary to folk-rock to folk-jazz, and was now about to drop the "folk."

Also, Joni seemed to be in better control of her loneliness. "I don't have a large circle of friends," she admitted. "I have a very few close friends and then there's a whole lot of people I'm sort of indifferent to. But there's other kinds of loneliness which are very beautiful. Like sometimes I go up to my land in British Columbia and spend time alone in the country surrounded by the beauty of natural things. There's a romance which accompanies it, so you generally don't feel self-pity. In the city, when you're surrounded by people who are continually interacting, the loneliness makes you feel like you've sinned. All around you you see lovers or families and you're alone, and you think: Why? What did I do to deserve this? That's why I think the cities are much lonelier than the country."

JOSEPH STEVENS, LONDON, 1974

47

48

At the end of her tour, Joni settled into a house in Bel Air with John Guerin, drummer for the L.A. Express. It's a large house, a sixteen-room hacienda in one of the most fashionable neighborhoods in Los Angeles. Joni and John live quietly, seeing a few friends, making a little music, playing a little cribbage. She appears to be content, dividing her time between the city of the angels and the house in Vancouver, where she retires to paint and write music. When she can, she visits Saskatoon to see her

parents. Joni's got the best of both worlds now, the stimulation of a large, dynamic city and the solitude of a place in the country. The Bel Air house contains a skylight studio at the top of a curving staircase. The room is furnished minimally—a couple of stools, an easel, and a large table that holds Joni's sketches and sketching paraphernalia. There is no mirror in the room; she finds them distracting in any place where she works.

Joni has kept journals for years, lovely books in which she practices her calligraphy, and illustrates her poems and thoughts with delicate, beautiful drawings. The notebooks are like Joni herself, bursting with creations, an artistic jumble of light and dark.

Although she is very Americanized, Joni still thinks of herself as a Canadian. "I definitely am Canadian. I'm proud of that and when it came to settling the place where I decided I wanted to spend my old years, I bought some property north of Vancouver.

"I think there is a lot of prairie in my music and in Neil Young's music as well. I think both of us have a striding quality to our music which is like long steps across flat land. I think so, although I'm getting a little New Yorkish now with this jazz influence that's coming in. It's got to be urbanized. I talk about American cities, about Paris, about Greece. I talk about the places where I am."

After her *Miles of Aisles* tour, folksinger Malka interviewed her, the first interview Joni had allowed in some time. "Do you ever envision or fear that the well of creativity might dry up?" she asked Joni.

"Well, every year for the last four years I have said, 'That's it.' I feel often that it has run dry, you know, and all of a sudden things just come pouring out. But I know, I know that this is a feeling that increases as you get older. I have a fear that I might become a tunesmith, that I would be able to write songs but not poetry. I don't know. It's a mystery, the creative process; inspiration is a mystery, but I think that as long as you still have questions the muse has got to be there. You throw a question out to the muses and maybe they drop something back on you."

"What are your aims now?" Joni was asked.

"Well, I really don't feel I've scratched the surface of my music. I'm not all that confident about my words. Thematically I think that I'm running out of things which I feel are important enough to describe verbally. I really think that as you get older life's experiences become more; I begin to see the paradoxes resolved. It's almost like most things that I would once dwell on and explore for an hour, I would shrug my shoulders to now. In your twenties, things are still profound and being uncovered. However, I think there's a way to keep that alive if you don't start putting up too many blocks. I feel that my music will continue to grow—I'm almost a pianist now, and the same thing with the guitar. And I also continue to draw, and that also is in a stage of growth. It hasn't stagnated yet. And I hope to bring all these things together.

"Another thing I'd like to do is make a film. There's a lot of things I'd like to do,

BRUCE DITCHFIELD. WITH JULIE AT AN LA EXPRESS CONCERT, SANTA BARBARA

so I still feel young as an artist. I don't feel like my best work is behind me. I feel as if it's still in front."

51

JONI MITCHELL — HER MUSIC

"The most important thing," said Joni Mitchell, "is to write in your own blood. I bare intimate feelings because people should know how other people feel."

"When Joni writes," said Judy Collins, who made Joni Mitchell's songs world-famous, "she finds the words that unthread the confusion and paints scenes as vivid and distinct as her watercolors. When she sings the circle is completed. Whether she sings in her stained-glass and dark wood house in Laurel Canyon or on the stage in multi-colored lights, Joni takes you on trips interwoven with magic and the secret of what it feels like to be a woman."

"Joni is the first woman to match any man on his own terms as a songwriter, guitar player, or as an incredibly magnetic human being." Those words are Linda Ronstadt's.

"I think that most of her stuff is stuff that any human can relate to in some way. If a man hasn't gone through it maybe he knows somebody who has," commented Tom Rush, who was the first star to sing Joni's music.

"Joni exorcises her demons by writing those songs," pointed out Stephen Stills, "and in so doing she reaches way down and grabs the essence of something very private and personal to women."

"You have to write for yourself," said Joni Mitchell. "If I express a truthful emotion that is pure and honest, then I consider the poem a success. If you are sad, then you should feel sad. The French are good at that. They show what they feel and in that way purge themselves of it."

When Joni came into the music business, it was dominated by men and by heavy, masculine music. In the songs themselves, women were never equal companions; instead they were either cold-hearted bitches or motherly creatures who offered hot food and warm beds. But the singer-hero usually carried his own sleeping bag, as a sign he was "movin' on." It was axiomatic; woman represented stability and ties; man was creativity and freedom. It was woman who was left behind, and man who did the leaving. Joni's lyrics changed all that. Although the search for love is a central theme in the Mitchell songs, she was also on a search for freedom; woman has as much need to seek the freedom to be creative as man has.

53

"Freedom to me is the luxury of being able to follow the path of the heart," Joni has said. "I think that's the only way that you maintain the magic in your life, that you keep your child alive. Freedom is necessary for me in order to create, and if I don't create I don't feel alive."

It is important to keep in mind, when one analyzes Joni Mitchell's music, that there are three strong yet paradoxical strains in her personality, each of them affecting her work. The first, bred into her by her mother, is a strain of old-fashioned domesticity.

"We Canadians are a bit more nosegay, more old-fashioned bouquet than Americans. We're poets because we're such a *reminiscent* kind of people. My poetry is urbanized and Americanized but my music is influenced by the prairies. When I was a kid, my mother used to take me out to the fields to teach me bird calls. There was a lot of space behind individual sounds. People in the city are so accustomed to hearing a jumble of different sounds that when they come to making music, they fill it up with all sorts of different things."

Joni often expresses her affection in homey, traditional female ways. Said Graham Nash when they were living together, "Joni bakes better pies than Myrtle"; he was referring to Joni's mother. Sandra Shevey wrote: "Joni is a wholly creative person. If she is not writing, she is painting, weaving, working in enamel. She makes lovely jewelry. She's finished a wardrobe of simple, A-line dresses, and she has begun to knit scarves on planes to keep from smoking. Joni sees her friends in shades of colors and has made for them appropriate mufflers. 'Cass's [the late Mama Cass Elliot] is bright, gypsy colors. Graham Nash's is darker tones: purple, black, forest green. Elliot's [Roberts] is dusty: brown, navy, rust, gray.'"

When a reporter for *Time* magazine, David DeVoss, visited her in her new Bel Air home for an interview in 1974, Joni cooked him a lavish dinner. "Three meticulously cooked courses," including Yorkshire pudding like her mother used to make and spiced apple dumplings. Calling the kitchen "the best room in the house,"

54

Joni added, "Maybe I'm growing old, but I enjoy taking care of this place."

"I'm a very romantic person," Joni told *Music World* in 1973. "I like fresh flowers and things like that around. I think there's a lack of romance in everything today. Women are being misguided. The people who are guiding them in fashion are homosexual, therefore you get fashions that are extremely masculine, either to make a woman look foolish or to make it easier for men to look like women. It's like . . . for a long time I couldn't go out without wearing false eyelashes. Now that's really silly. It really is a man's world, you know?"

As a resident of this "man's world," Joni wrote lyrics of extreme beauty and poignancy, expressing herself in the traditional "old lady's" role, that of a submissive and understanding lover to a difficult ramblin' man. In "Chelsea Morning," she promises delights of all kinds if only her lover will stay. In "Conversation," another song about unrequited love, she brings her beloved apples and cheeses, while he brings her songs to play. And he sees her only when he pleases. "Willy is my child, he is my father," she writes in a song for Graham Nash, "I would be his lady all my life."

In *Blue*, perhaps her most personal album, Joni sets out a list of services that she would gladly perform for her lover: she wants to talk to him, shampoo him, renew him again and again; she wants to write him a love letter, knit him a sweater, make him feel better, make him feel free. Over and over in her earlier albums, Joni plays or offers to play the traditional game of woman-giver and man-taker.

Yet, supplementing this strain of traditional domesticity, there is a strain of wildness, of rebellion, in Joni, dating back to her earliest years in Saskatchewan.

"It was then and still is a constant war to liberate myself from values not applicable to the period in which I live," she said not long ago, a summation of feelings she had long held. "Alive, alive, I want to get up and jive; I want to wreck my stockings in some juke box jive," she writes in "All I

JIM MARSHALL. LAUREL CANYON, 1971

Want." Joni is well-known to love "roses and kisses and all those pretty men to tell her all those pretty lies," as she herself has told us. A bottle of wine and good loving— Joni is the consummate lover; she operates on emotion rather than thought. "I have difficulty expressing myself when I want to be serious; I create by feeling rather than by intellectualizing," she once stated.

Predominant in Joni's songs is love, the joy of a new love, the pain of a love being destroyed, the disillusions of a past love. "Disappointment," she joked, "is a favorite theme of mine."

"Love is such a powerful force," she told Malka. "My main interest in life is human relationships and human interaction and the exchange of feelings, person to person, on a one-to-one basis, or on a larger basis projecting to an audience. Love is a peculiar feeling, because it's subject to so much . . . change. The way that love feels at the beginning of a relationship and the changes that it goes through, I keep asking myself, 'What is it?'

"It always seemed like a commitment to me when you said to someone, 'I love you,' or if they said that to you. It meant that you were there for them, and that you could trust them. But knowing from myself that I have said that and then reneged on it in the supportive—in the physical— sense, that I was no longer there side by side with that person. So I say, 'Well, does that cancel the feeling out? Did I really love? Or what is it?' I really believe that the maintenance of individuality is so necessary to what we would call a true or lasting love that people who say 'I love you' and then do a Pygmalion number on you are wrong, you know. Love has to encompass all of the things that a person is. Love is a very hard feeling to keep alive. It's a very fragile plant."

Joni the traditionalist, Joni the free lover, and the third strain—the strongest of all— Joni the creative artist who needs her freedom in order to do her best work, to keep the lines open between herself and her muse, a male muse she laughed about to *Time* magazine: His name is Art, and he lends her the key to what she calls "the shrine of creativity." "I feel like I'm mar-

ried to this guy named Art. I'm responsible to my Art above all else."

When *Time* asked her if she planned to marry again, she conceded that she probably would not. "My family consists of pieces of work that go out in the world. Instead of hanging around for nineteen years they leave the nest early," she smiled.

Time described Joni as "a modern Isadora whose life is a litmus for the innocent and imaginative"—pretty fancy verbiage for a country girl from Saskatoon who likes to dance to rock and roll. But, in essence, the words are correct. Isadora Duncan laid her personal life on the line for her Art, and danced a dance of freedom, and so does Joni with her music. Like the phoenix, Joni Mitchell arises renewed from the "smoke and ash" of her disappointments. She is stubborn, a survivor, candid and essentially pure of heart, and her songs reflect all of these. Although every old love is replaced by a new, Joni's wryness never gives way to cynicism. Although every new love turns to an old one, her optimism, even at her unhappiest, is never quenched. Above all, like Isadora, she reaches her audiences. They know her; they recognize her in themselves and themselves in her. Everybody loves, everybody suffers, everybody hopes, and everybody is lonely. Joni distills these themes in poem-portraits that give her listeners that immediate shock of recognition that stamps a work of art.

"Everyone seems to know Joni," wrote *Time*. "She is the rural neophyte waiting in a subway, a free spirit drinking wine in the moonlight, an organic Earth Mother dispensing fresh bread and herb tea, and the reticent feminist who by trial and error has charted the male as well as the female ego."

Joni's themes are love, its joys and disappointments; success, its joys and disappointments; and freedom, *its* joys and disappointments. Intensely personal and autobiographical, her songs have charted her development from a city-shy Canadian girl into a mature woman of heart and mind, although still hoping for that magical love that will at the same time bind her and free her. To listen to her first six albums in sequence is to share a trip through Joni's own life, from those first post-Chuck Mitchell days in Greenwich Village to the Laurel Canyon house and the Hollywood scene, to Crete, to Paris, and finally, to isolated, peaceful Vancouver, as Joni Mitchell went about finding out who she was.

In her first album, *Song to a Seagull* (Reprise 6293), Joni set down themes that

would carry on throughout her work, developing from album to album: the conflict between love and freedom; the broken promises of elusive lovers; a love-hate relationship with the city; the anxieties and

ambiguities of the search for love, success, and an end to loneliness. Indifferently produced by David Crosby, *Seagull* featured Joni on acoustic guitar and piano, her voice breathy and not always fully assured. Yet it was not an unworthy introduction to Joni's own artistry, because it was beautifully programmed in the autobiographical way that became the Mitchell trademark. "I Came to the City" she called Side One; it introduced the listener to a newly divorced but not bitter Joni in "I Had a King." She had a king in a salt-rusted carriage who carried her off to his country for marriage too soon. Now she can't go back there anymore, because her keys won't fit the door. Yet she recognizes that there's no one to blame, only the "power of moons."

"Michael from Mountains," previously recorded by Judy Collins, is Joni's portrait of the boy-man who is called away by his own fantasies from the girl who loves him. "He needs you to care and you know you do . . . you want to know all, but his mountains have called so you never do." Told gently and without heaviness, it's a story that Joni would tell again and again, a story of conflicting dreams that pull lovers apart.

"Marcie" is the first song-painting in the Mitchell gallery of ladies who have lost their lovers and who cannot hack it alone. "Marcie's faucet needs a plumber, Marcie's sorrow needs a man," she tells us sadly, sympathetically.

"Nathan La Franeer" sums up all Joni's negative feelings toward the big city, "the ghostly garden." Nathan is the surly New York cabby who drives the singer "from confusion to the plane" in "the bedlam of the day." Nathan's curses and grumbles, his enraged hand reaching out for more money, symbolize the senseless, misdirected hostilities bred in a city's dirt, noise, and confinement. It makes her happy to leave the town behind for the seaside.

The second half of the album Joni calls "Out of the City and Down to the Seaside." It begins with a gently ironic yet idyllic description of life in the antithesis of New York City—Sisotowbell Lane—which you must "wade through the wheat" to get to, and where you can sit in a rocking chair and eat "muffin buns and berries."

In "The Dawntreader," Joni's talent for painting is obvious in her descriptive, colorful phrases, like "Peridots and periwinkle blue medallions; gilded galleons spilled across the ocean floor"—these are visual as well as verbal images.

"The Pirate of Penance" tells a familiar story, that of a girl abandoned by a lover whose thirst for freedom is deeper than his need for love, and "Song to a Seagull," previously recorded by Buffy Sainte-Marie, is a paean to dreams and to freedom: "My dreams with the seagulls fly, out of reach, out of cry."

But it is in the last song of the album, "Cactus Tree," which Joni called "a grocery list of men I've liked, or loved, or left behind," that Joni declares for personal freedom over an involving love, rejecting her suitors because "she's so busy being free." There is an irony in this song; Joni seems to know that she is giving up something important in exchange for this freedom.

"I feel my music with a solitary voice and a solitary guitar," Joni told the New York

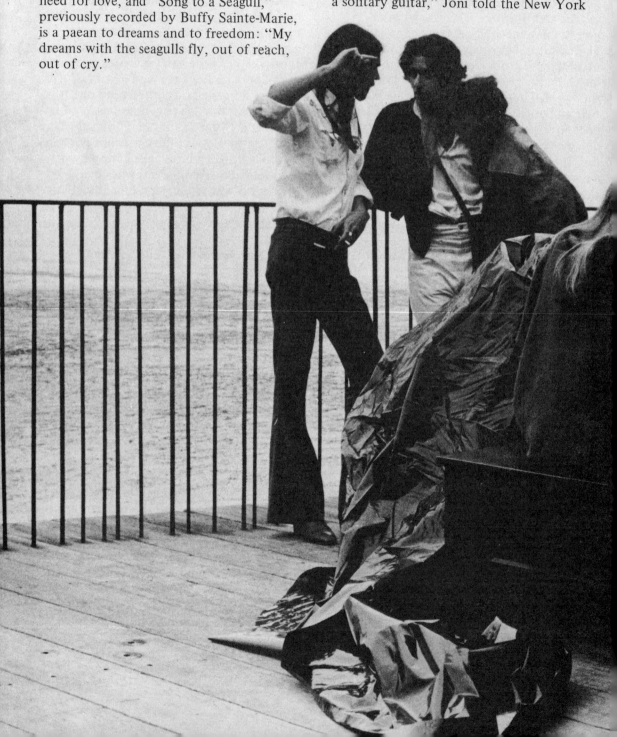

Times shortly after her first album was released. "I'm more prolific with melodies than with words, but quite often I write poems and then set them to music. I guess I'm primarily an artist; what I like best is making new music. It's like going into a trance; I sit down with a melody and reminisce. I find it easier to think about my feelings in retrospect. The way I'd like to work from now on is to go into a studio as soon as a song is finished, when the feeling of the song is most intense; you should record songs when you believe them the most."

Joni's artistry on her first album was surprisingly mature. Joni herself was deprecating about her voice and her voice training. "I had none," she explained to *Rolling Stone*. "I used to be a breathy little soprano. Then one day I found that I could sing low. At first I thought that I had lost my voice forever. I could either sing a breathy high part or a raspy low part. Then the two came together by themselves. It was uncomfortable for a while but I worked it out, and now I've got this voice."

Rolling Stone defined "this voice" as a "fluttery but controlled kind of soprano, the kind that can slide effortlessly from the middle register to piercing highs in mid-word." *Music World* called Joni's voice "airbrushed gold leaf"; and *Cue*, in an ecstatically favorable review of her work, waxed positively poetic:

"Richly modal, it is pervaded by an exotic calmness, reminding one of things like wind chimes or the glass globes Japanese fishermen use to float their nets. Against this delicate background her reedy voice with its natural vibrato is free to discover its own paths of harmony . . . suddenly, like a hawk on an updraft, she will carve a breathtaking harmonic arc and soar out over the landscape of her verse."

Joni's voice was matched by her poetry, which, she has admitted more than once, was heavily influenced by Leonard Cohen—Canadian poet, singer, and songwriter ("Suzanne," "Sisters of Mercy," and many others). "I love Leonard's sentiments, so I've been strongly influenced by him. Knowing Leonard has made me even more demanding of myself. He sets new standards for people—like running the minute mile. He taught me to really work on the poignancy of a story."

Her guitar work was as unusual as her lyrics and her strange, swooping, changeable voice. David Crosby, ex-Byrd, soon to be a member of Crosby, Stills, and Nash, produced her first album and helped her to develop a complex and difficult method of guitar tuning that made her music unique and hard to copy. She often had to retune between songs and at least two of her songs, "The Dawntreader" and "I Don't Know Where I Stand," cannot be played at all on a normally tuned guitar.

Independent, Joni had not included her two best-known songs, "Both Sides Now" and "The Circle Game," on her first album. It was as though she wasn't sure they still belonged to her. Top entertainers of every stripe had recorded "Both Sides Now"—everybody from Judy Collins to Bing Crosby and Frank Sinatra. Of the more than twenty versions of the song, Joni herself likes Dave Van Ronk's the most. "He brings another quality to the song. He gives it a man's touch, a feeling of male sadness," she commented.

"Most of my songs are about myself, songs of personal experience. It's very important to me how I sing them. But it's funny—after a song's been written, it becomes a whole different thing; you don't own it anymore. I love to hear men sing my

songs, because they're written from a feminine point of view, and men bring totally different things to them."

Joni's second album, *Clouds* (Reprise 6341), carries the dedication, "For Sadie J. McKee," Joni's grandmother, "who loved Robbie Burns and minor-key music and married a farmer who didn't understand." The album marked her debut as producer of her own recorded music, a role she has kept to this day.

"I was working with a producer, and we were pulling each other in opposite directions. I was working within this framework of sound equipment, and the sound was fantastic, but I felt stifled. Now the sound isn't so good, but at least I know I'm doing what I want to do," she declared.

An album that "gets into the pain of the heart," in Joni's words, *Clouds* shows many of the faces of love. Once again, it is the listener, Joni, and her guitar that form a simple triangle filled with powerfully evocative lyrics and complex, plaintive melodies.

There are two songs that recreate her love affair with Leonard Cohen, "That Song about the Midway," in which the lover appears as "a devil wearing wings," and "The Gallery," in which he is a self-styled saint.

In "Tin Angel," Joni has found a new love, but he has no heart, only sorrow in his eyes like "an angel made of tin." She has been waiting for a Golden Prince, but she accepts this man who is "dark with darker moods," because she is a woman who must love somebody always.

Clouds is an album of incredibly rich melody, drenched in the butterscotch sunlight of "Chelsea Morning," dark with the somber blueness of the flowers and the woman in "Roses Blue." In "I Don't Know Where I Stand," Joni states a universal problem of the heart, being afraid to be the first to say "I love you." She is again allowing the man to dictate the terms of the relationship. But other fears are discarded in "I Think I Understand," an upbeat song of optimism—the conquering of a troubled mind, of uncertainty and darkness, by the light of self-knowledge.

In "The Fiddle and the Drum," Joni made her first and perhaps her last political statement. Not a protest singer, Joni's voice was generally unraised for causes, although she felt strongly about environmental protection. "It's good to be exposed to politics and what's going down here," she told *Rolling Stone*, "but it does damage to me. Too much of it can cripple me. And if I really let myself think about it—the violence, the sickness, all of it—I think I'd flip out."

And, even in her antiwar song, her approach is gentle, as tender as a mother's chiding: "And so once again, Oh America, my friend . . . you are fighting us all . . . But we can remember all the good things you are . . . and so we ask you please, can we help you find the peace and the star?" This is the same attitude she takes in "Woodstock," when she urges us all back to our state of innocence in the garden.

Joni's painting has never been more beautiful than on the album cover of *Clouds*. Here is the Magic Princess, flowing golden hair, clutching a medieval day lily. Behind

GEORGE LANGE

her, reflected in the moat by the dying rays of the red and gold setting sun, is her castle, lights ablaze. Her self-portrait, and the castle, make the perfect setting for the last song on the album, Joni's most celebrated hit, "Both Sides Now." It's a song that celebrates both the ups and downs of life, its realities and illusions, its disappointments as well as its joys. For a Joni Mitchell song, it is remarkably easy to sing, well within the range of even the amateur, and its lyrics strike a responsive chord in every breast. For which of us has not looked at life from both sides now, eaten of the bitter as well as drunk of the sweet?

With *Clouds*, Joni came into full control of her albums. Not only did she write and sing all of the songs herself, but she painted the album cover and produced the recording. It was a remarkable display of versatility, especially since she performed every task so professionally, even with touches of genius. Her painter's eye colors her lyrics, her musician's ear makes her paintings flow like melodies, and her guitar ties a ribbon of song around the listener, to draw him closer to the words, and to the unfolding of Joni's personal history.

Ladies of the Canyon (Reprise 6376) is the most diverse of all of Joni's albums; it touches all the bases. Joni added piano, which she played herself, a cello, clarinet, flute, percussion, and baritone saxophone. "The Lookout Mountain United Down-

stairs Choir" sang the chorus on "The Circle Game." The educated guesser at once identified them as Messrs. Crosby, Stills, Nash, and Young.

Joni examines the realities of love in several of the songs on the album. In "Willy," written for Graham Nash, she sings of a woman who loves a man who wants to run away and hide, because he's afraid to feel. Yet the woman's dominant emotion is hope—she feels as though she's just being born, "like a shiny light breaking in a storm." In "Conversation," she tells the age-old story of a woman in love with a man who is tied to another, a man who treats her only as a friend and confidante. Again, the singer is passive, hopeful, waiting. And in "Blue Boy," the woman is in love with a man made of stone, knowing that, if she allows the relationship to continue on his terms, he will turn her to stone as well.

"Rainy Night House" is a tender farewell to Leonard Cohen, the "holy man on the FM radio," who gave up "all the golden factories" to learn his psychic identity. It is a gentle, nostalgic, and loving song, sung without bitterness, even though it was she who was left behind in the quest.

"For Free" is Joni's tongue-in-cheek look at her success and her affluence. Now she plays only for money and those "velvet curtain calls," while a one-man band by the quick lunch stand plays real good . . . and for free. It was the first statement of a theme that would be a prevalent one in future albums—the underside of success and its responsibilities.

The title song, "Ladies of the Canyon," paints lyric-portraits of three kinds of Laurel Canyon ladies, California types of the late sixties in their antique finery and brightly colored beads. Each of them, all of them, could be Joni herself, with her well-fed cats, her handicrafts, her music. All of them are aspects of her own nature.

"Woodstock," recorded also by Crosby, Stills, Nash, and Young, struck the note on which the psychedelic sixties ended. A celebration of the greatest music festival ever held, an occasion of peace and love, "Woodstock" was the symbol of the dawning age of Aquarius, and the song defined Joni's

generation. "Stardust, golden" were these children of Woodstock, but their innocence was lost; was it possible to retrieve it? The song says yes, "life is for learning."

Joni's sassy look at ecological blight, "Big Yellow Taxi," is the ultimate word on the subject, Paradise bulldozed and turned into a parking lot. No more spots on the apples, but no more birds and bees, either, and all the trees in a museum. Sung in a rollicking tempo, "Taxi" carried a heavy message in a light style. Bob Dylan would sing it years later; he always considered Joni's work top-drawer.

"The Circle Game," another often-recorded Mitchell song, is the lyricist's commentary on the passage of life, the changing dreams of youth and middle age, and the inevitability of death. Time is a carousel on which we are all riding as "the painted ponies go up and down." We are all captive, we can only go on into the future, looking behind.

Yet these lines seem to be contradicted by the words of "The Arrangement," in which she reproves the successful subur-banite. "You could have been more than a name on the door," she tells him, and urges him to break away and find a better life while there is still time. But she knows that he won't; he is too comfortable with his cars and his bars and his credit cards; it's only a Gauguin who can leave a bank at the age of thirty-five to go to the South Seas and paint.

Once again, Joni provided the artwork for the album cover, a simple portrait of herself, done in one continuous line, and a colorful fragment of Laurel Canyon, show-ing her little house and a bright red car. "The drawings, the music, and the words are very much tied together," she admitted, for she herself was the quintessential "Lady of the Canyon"—earth mother, nurturer, "old Lady," lover, artist—what Ellen Willis once described as "the compleat hippie chick."

"It's like taste," Joni continued. "It changes and reflects in everything you do creatively. I never get frustrated to where I'll say: 'quit writing.' I come to dry periods where either I feel I don't have anything new to say or feel like I'm repeating patterns.

"The kind of material I want to write—I

want it to be brighter, to get people up, to grab people. So I'm stifling any feelings of solitude or certain moods I might ordinarily develop into a song. I steer away from that now because I don't want that kind of material to perform."

Years after *Ladies of the Canyon* had become a part of musical history, Joni was asked how she felt her old albums stood up. She gave this answer, and it was an honest and objective look at her work: "I don't enjoy some of the old records; I see too much of my growing stage. I've changed my point of view too much. There are some of them I can still bring life to, but some that I can't. Let's take the *Ladies of the Canyon* album—there are good songs on there which I feel still stand up and which I could still sing. There's a song called 'The Arrangement' which seemed to me a fore-runner and I think has more musical sophistication than anything else on the album. And the *Blue* album, for the most part, holds up. But there are some early songs where there is too much naiveté in some of the lyrics for me to be able now to project convincingly."

"Sorrow is so easy to express and yet so hard to tell," Joni once wrote. And she discussed loneliness with her friend Malka:

"I suppose people have always been lonely but this, I think, is an especially lonely time to live in. So many people are valueless or confused. I know a lot of guilty people who are living a very open kind of free life who don't really believe that what they're doing is right, and their defense to that is to totally advocate what they're doing, as if it were right, but somewhere deep in them they're confused. Things change so rapidly. Relationships don't seem to have any longevity. Occasionally you see people who have been together for six or seven, maybe twelve years, but for the most part people drift in and out of relationships continually. There isn't a lot of commitment to anything; it's a disposable society."

Loneliness and broken relationships are the subject of *Blue* (Reprise 2038), the album that marked Joni's return to the public after a withdrawal of almost two years. Depressed, miserably unhappy, disillusioned

JONI MITCHELL

by love and by media curiosity and speculation about her love life, Joni had stopped concertizing and gone off on a series of travels to new countries, in search of herself. But she didn't stop writing, and *Blue* shows a sensitivity and a poetry, a vulnerability unmatched by lesser artists. Her voice on this album swoops and soars from the low to the highest registers, sometimes in mid-note, like the wail of an abandoned lover. The piano, which can be a dark and lonely instrument, comes to the forefront on this album; Joni was thinking more of piano than guitar in her songwriting now.

As romantically sad as the album is, it

JIM MARSHALL

64

is filled with friends and former lovers. Stephen Stills, who played bass on Joni's first album, *Song to a Seagull*, plays both bass and guitar on this one; James Taylor plays guitar on three songs. (Joni had sung with Taylor on the cut "Long Ago, Far Away" on Taylor's own album, *Mud Slide Slim*. And together they had sung with Carole King on a number of songs on Carole's album, *Tapestry*. In fact, it was James Taylor who had introduced Joni to Carole.)

Aside from the piano and guitars, Joni employed only pedal steel and drums on the album, Sneeky Pete on pedal and Russ Kunkel on drums. They helped to provide the frisky Latin and Calypso beats that underscore the songs so paradoxically, when Joni sings of heartbreak in clap-your-hands tempos.

The story of the album revolves around "Blue," her lost lover (Graham Nash), with a few affectionate looks at another lover, James Taylor. Taylor is "Carey," who is "the bright red devil who keeps me in this tourist town" on Crete. He's a "mean old daddy," but Joni likes him fine and tells him so with affection. In "California," Joni, who had met "a redneck on a Grecian isle" (James), wants to come back to a warm land, California, not one which is "old and cold and settled in its ways." Yet, unhappiness continues to dog her, for once back in California she longs to leave again. "It don't snow here, it stays pretty green," she laments, longing for an ice-covered river "I could skate away on."

But it's in the five main songs on the album, those written for Graham, that Joni allows her deepest feelings to show. They are among the most beautiful love songs ever composed. In "All I Want," a song for the beginning of a love, Joni is looking for a love that will set her free, set her lover free, bring out the best in both of them. It's a long and lonely road that she's been traveling, and she hopes it has come to an end, leaving her in the land of the living, happy, alive, and free. But it cannot happen, at least not permanently.

In "My Old Man," she sings the same kind of love song that Bessie Smith made famous: he gives me good lovin' and when he goes away my bed is too big and the fryin' pan is too wide. It's a woman's song, the traditional blues lament for a man who is free to come and go while the woman stays behind; when he turns up, the days and nights are bright, but when he's gone, everything is dark and gloomy.

"A Case of You" is the artist-poet's song to a man she's entirely hung up on, a man in her blood like holy wine. "Oh, I am a lonely painter, I live in a box of paints," and "I drew a map of Canada, with your face sketched on it twice." Her lover has given her assurances: "I am as constant as the northern star; love is touching souls." But their love got lost along the way, leaving Joni with his image in her blood, he tasting so bitter and so sweet, that she could drink a case of him and still be on her feet. But that's just a hope; for she isn't on her feet now, she's way, way down with those lonesome blues.

In "This Flight Tonight," Joni has left him. Although he has the lovin' that leaves her weak, he also has that look so critical that she cannot communicate with him. She has opted for "out," for freedom, but the pain is intense and all she can think of is that she shouldn't be here, on this plane; she should be with her baby, even though she sometimes thinks love is just mythical.

Mythical perhaps, but food and drink for Joni Mitchell. She has looked for love, has found it, and it has destroyed her once again. In "Blue," the title song on the album and the saddest, she tells her audience a little of how it happened. She has wanted permanence, even marriage. "You know I've been to sea before," she says. "Crown and anchor me or let me sail away." What has come between herself and her lover, what has made the waves so high it was impossible to sail through them? Acid, booze and ass, needles, guns and grass. Although Joni doesn't share her contemporaries' fascination with hell ("the hippest way to go") she has gone down into it for Blue's sake, because she loves him. It doesn't work —it cannot work—and so she leaves him a

gift, the sweetest in her possession, a shell filled with a lullabye. There is so much pain and gentleness in this song that tears spring to the eyes when you listen to it.

Blue turned a lot of people's heads around; it was such a departure from Joni's folk-art style; it could perhaps be best described as folk-blues. *For the Roses*, Joni's first album for David Geffen's label, Asylum (Asylum 0598), was folk-rock, and the influence of Los Angeles and its rock and roll music was felt throughout the album.

"My music now is becoming more rhythmic," she'd told *Rolling Stone*. "It's because I'm in Los Angeles and my friends are mostly rock and roll people . . . and being influenced by that rhythm. I've always liked it. When I was in Saskatchewan, I loved to dance," she grinned.

The melodies on *For the Roses* are far less complex and subtle than anything Joni had written before. "I don't notice what I'm doing so much until I've done it and then look back at it. At the time, you're really not aware you're doing it.

"In order to be simplified it has to be honed down more. It takes a lot more polishing for that simplicity than it did for anything complicated. I do a lot of night-writing. I need solitude to write. I used to be able to write under almost any conditions but not anymore 'cause I have to go

STUART BRATESMAN. NEW HAMPSHIRE PRIMARY, 1972

inside myself so far, to search through a theme.

"First of all, I'll write something down and then I think: Oh, I like how the words sound together but it doesn't say anything. When I finish a new song I take it and play it for my friends, who are fine musicians and writers. I'm very impressed by their reactions to it. If they like it, I'm knocked out. I guess I write for those people. They're really my audience."

If Joni's melodies were simpler, catchier on *For the Roses*, her voice matched them. For years her detractors were put off by the intensity of her vocalizing and her sudden changes in pitch and key. Now, many new fans were won, as Joni kept her voice lower and more cool, singing with and not against her accompaniment. She added Tommy Scott on woodwinds and reeds, Bobby Notkoff on strings, Wilton Felder on bass, Ross Kunkel on drums, Bobbye Hall on percussion, Graham Nash again on harmonica, James Burton on electric guitar, and, on "Blonde in the Bleachers," Stephen Stills's rock and roll band.

With this album, Joni had a new success: a hit single, as "You Turn Me On, I'm a Radio" worked its way up the Top Forty charts. *For the Roses* was almost an album of popular song, although far superior to the general run of such albums. Again, Joni was taking risks with her personal life, filling in the details of her musical self-portrait, but there was a strong new note being sounded. "I am a woman of heart and mind," she sang, "looking for affection and respect, a little passion." In this love affair, which once again seems not to be working out, Joni takes a stronger stance than ever before. Seeing her lover clearly for what he is, a man on "the empty side," Joni has come light years from "Tin Angel" on her first album. She will *try* to be there for him, she promises, but she holds her deepest self in reserve; you can tell she's ready to split.

In "Let the Wind Carry Me," a song of youthful rebellion, Joni tells us that sometimes she wants to settle down and raise up somebody's child, but the feeling passes and leaves her like a wild seed, content for the wind to carry her anywhere.

If there is any unifying theme on *For the Roses*, it is: lessons learned. Each song is a mature echo of something that troubled Joni in her scuffling days. In "Blonde in the Bleachers," she has learned that "you can't hold the hand of a rock and roll man very long," and heaven knows Joni had tried! In "Banquet," the darkling song that opens this album, Joni tells us that life is something found in a fortune cookie: some people get to taste it all, some a little bit, and others are left with nothing. "Some turn to Jesus and some turn to heroin," she says, and she has known and loved men who've turned to both.

She's learned a lot about success, too. The title song, "For the Roses," examines success in the music business and finds that it has its spotty side. "Up the charts . . . everything's first class . . . people who have slices of you from the company . . ." Who knows if you can do it again? With unbearable sweetness, she asks: "Remember the days when you used to sit and make up your tunes for love?" a poignant echo of "For Free." Consensus has it that Joni wrote this for James Taylor, but one feels that she herself stands at the center of this song, in the winner's circle, having run for the roses and won . . . for now. "Just when you're getting a taste for worship, they start bringing out the hammers and the boards and the nails." She's been there if anybody has.

There are new metaphors on this album —electricity, fire, static. "Sweet fire calling," she sings in "Cold Steel and Sweet Fire," the best song on heroin addiction since Leonard Cohen's "Dress Rehearsal Rag"— it's even better than "Sister Morphine" by the Stones. Cohen's lines, "And isn't it a long way down? And isn't it a strange way down?" become Mitchell's "Down, down, down the dark ladder," and a searing wail of the clarinet.

"You've got to roar like forest fire, you've got to spread your light like blazes," she sings in "Judgment of the Moon and Stars (Ludwig's Tune)," a hymn to creativity and its loneliness, inspired by a book Joni had read, *Ludwig von Beethoven's Spiritual Awakening*. Beethoven, deaf, "raw," alone, is the epitome of the creative

artist who faces pain and derision but must ignore it and go his own path, surmounting with his art his personal unhappiness.

"I'd like to see you sometime," she tells "Sweet Baby James" with pert independence. "I spring from the boulders like a mama lion. I'm not ready to change my name again . . . I'd just like to see you sometime." This is cooler than she has been in any of her songs. She has most of all learned a *lesson in survival*. The spirit inside her is not timid, although sometimes timidity shows, and she knows her needs. Knows them and will fulfill them. She can't lead her lover's life, even though the alternative is loneliness.

"Barangrill" is a wry fantasy; waitresses, Joni seems to be saying, know where it's at; they don't trouble themselves with anxieties, or with choices—split or stay? They just think about their boyfriends and do eggs over easy. That's the life, she sings with a shake of her head, knowing the fantasy for what it is. There's a funny story connected with "Barangrill." Joni wanted a third verse to the song, but hadn't come up with one. Driving home from the studio late at night, she stopped at a service station where a black attendant, learning that she was a singer, told her that he was a singer, too, and could sing like Nat King Cole. To Joni's delight, he sang to her, improvising verses about his work. And she made the third verse up about him: "The guy at the gaspumps, he's got a lot of soul . . . he sings . . . just like Nat King Cole . . . about whitewalls and windshields and this job he's got." And he sings so good that you forget to ask about this mythical land of eternal peace called Barangrill, where nobody has to make difficult choices. It's a happy song, and the flute of Tommy Scott provides the perfect accompaniment for it.

Court and Spark (Asylum 7E-1001) moved Joni into the front rank of superstars and crowned her the queen of rock and roll. Her first platinum album, it offered three hit singles, "Raised on Robbery," "Help Me," and "Free Man in Paris." In addition, it was the first time that Joni had recorded a song she had not written herself. It was "Twisted," a golden oldie by Annie Ross and Wardell Grey, that Joni's

favorites Lambert, Hendricks, and Ross had sung years before.

Court and Spark flowed more freely than any of her earlier albums; Joni's voice sounded more relaxed and confident than ever, and kept more to the lower registers. And her attitude toward love seemed to have undergone yet a further change. Now, self-mockery appeared to be the keynote.

NEAL PRESTON. 1973

RICK SMOLAN, 1974

Analyzing the "struggle for higher positions and their search for love that sticks around," a familiar theme of Joni's, she sends up a prayer: "Send me somebody who's strong, and somewhat sincere," she begs.

And in "Just Like This Train," she sings: "I'm always running behind the time . . . shaking into town with the brakes complaining. I used to count lovers like railroad cars . . . lately I don't count on nothing, I just let things slide."

She no longer can give up everything for love; her own needs and her desire for freedom are now too completely entrenched. "The more he talked to me, the more he reached me," she sings in the title song, "Court and Spark." But Joni cannot give up L.A., the city of the fallen angels.

And in "Help Me," she recognizes immediately that she is falling in love with the wrong guy (again) and that love is trouble (again) but this time he's in as much danger as she is. "Both of us flirtin' around . . . hurtin' too. We love our lovin' . . . but not like we love our freedom." Joni has been in this situation many times . . . with a rambler and a gambler and a sweet-talking ladies'

man . . . but this time her freedom is uppermost in her mind.

In "Down to You," Joni examines the freedom of choice that is still left to somebody who, out of loneliness, runs to one-night stands and pickups in singles bars. She talks to the "constant stranger" who, craving warmth and beauty, settles for "something less than fascination." It's down to you. It's your choice after all. Even when love is gone, when the only thing left is sorrow and momentary pleasure, it comes down to you. "You're a brute, you're an angel. You can crawl, you can fly." Freedom is there.

Freedom is also the theme of "Free Man in Paris," an obvious reference to David Geffen, once her traveling companion. Here it is success and not love that keeps someone tied down—an umbilical cord made of telephone wires, a ball and chain created of deals, schemes, and money-making.

"Car on a Hill" is a bittersweet song in which Joni, once again, seems to have been abandoned. She sits and waits for the sound of his car and thinks about how good a love

affair is at the beginning . . . so much laughter and spark and sweetness in the dark. Yet, it's not a blue song, or a long lament, but a brief, even breezy jazzy ditty. Freedom blows like a wind right through it. You can tell that the end of this relationship will not find Joni broken and bleeding. Now she has turned her hangups into pref-

And I'm very tempted to go in that direction experimentally." Thus she spoke a couple of years before *Court and Spark*, showing what direction her music was heading in. Now, with the release of this album, which sold more than a million copies, she had reached that goal. Her voice was stronger, gutsier, and so were her music and lyrics.

erences; she will search for love again and again, but she no longer seems to count on finding it.

Backed by the L.A. Express (Tom Scott on woodwinds and reeds; Max Bennett on bass; John Guerin on drums and percussion) and by all-star friends like David Crosby and Graham Nash, Jose Feliciano, Robbie Robertson, Cheech & Chong, and Joe Sample, *Court and Spark* has a slicker sound than the earlier albums, and more of an ensemble feel. Joni has moved here almost to folk-jazz; on her next album she would go much further into "mellow listening." The harmonies and arrangements of *Court and Spark* are a far cry from the simple acoustic guitar she brought to her first album, or the reedy, breathy soprano folkie voice. This is a sophisticated album, a studio masterpiece.

"I've got a voice I haven't used yet and haven't developed, which is very deep and strong and could carry over a loud band.

Her innocence may have vanished, but what had come to take its place was strength and knowledge. Joni was now truly a woman of heart and mind.

Now that Joni had found her new sound, she developed it by taking it out on the road. In 1974, backed by an expanded L.A. Express—Tom Scott, Max Bennett, John Guerin, Robben Ford on electric guitar, and Larry Nash on piano—Joni went on a seventy-two-concert tour that took her down literal miles of aisles and resulted in a live double album, *Miles of Aisles* (Asylum AB 202), recorded at four of the West Coast concerts. There are eighteen numbers on the four sides, sixteen of them Mitchell standards decked out in new trappings and two of them—"For Love or Money" and "Jericho"—new songs. Five of the songs had appeared on *Ladies of the Canyon* ("Rainy Night House," "Big Yellow Taxi," "The Circle Game," "Woodstock," and "For Free"); five were from *Blue*

("A Case of You," "Blue," "All I Want," "Carey," and "The Last Time I Saw Richard"); three from *For the Roses* ("You Turn Me On, I'm a Radio," "Cold Blue Steel and Sweet Fire," "A Woman of Heart and Mind"); and one apiece from *Clouds* ("Both Sides Now"), *Song to a Seagull* ("Cactus Tree"), and *Court and Spark* ("People's Parties").

Clearly, Joni was leaving her oldest work behind. When she played the Nassau Coliseum in the late summer of 1974, the usual crowd called out to her the usual requests for the usual songs, her old hits. Shaking her head, Joni called back to them, "Would you ask Picasso to re-paint his Blue Period?" And, on the album, much the same thing can be heard. As Joni is retuning her guitar, you can hear the calls for "California," "Carey," and other songs.

"All right," says Joni with a comic drawl. "There's one thing that's always been like a major difference to me between the performing arts and being a painter. A painter does a painting, and he does a painting. That's it. He's had the joy of creating it and he hangs it on some wall and somebody buys it and somebody buys it again or maybe nobody buys it and it sits up in a loft somewhere till he dies. But nobody ever said to Van Gogh, 'Paint a *Starry Night* again, man.' He painted it and that's *it*!" Not only was the simile instantly recognizable, but it's significant that Joni identifies herself still very strongly with painting.

Joni herself played piano, guitar, and dulcimer on the tour and on the album. But where she used to stand alone on the stage, her breathy voice the delicate vessel that carried the feeling to an enraptured, silent audience, now she bopped to the jivin' jazz of her backup band, and toes started tapping. Joni had come a long way from the Newport Folk Festival days, and she had brought her audience with her every step of the way.

With the release, in fall of 1975, of Joni's eighth album, *The Hissing of Summer Lawns* (Asylum 7E-1051), she has come to a place in her music where the word "folk" no longer applies. *Summer Lawns* is a carefully constructed, no longer spontaneous kind of music, a studio recording with heavy jazz

and piano-bar vibes. It is the kind of music she'd explored in *Court and Spark* and concertized in *Miles of Aisles*, here brought to fruition. The compositions on *Summer Lawns* are again Joni's alone, with the exception of two: "Centerpiece" by Johnny Mandel and Jon Hendricks of Joni's old favorite group, Lambert, Hendricks and Ross; and "The Hissing of Summer Lawns," which Joni wrote with John Guerin, L.A. Express drummer and her old man.

Her backup band on this album is taken partly from L.A. Express (Max Bennett, Robben Ford, Victor Feldman, and John Guerin, but without Tom Scott) and partly from the Jazz Crusaders (Larry Carlton,

cycle it appears to be—is in the main far less personal and confessional than one has come to expect from Mitchell; she is obviously in the process of changing all her trademarks.

She herself must have sensed a possible puzzlement on the part of her fans, for her dedication of this album is so long and so rambling as to be almost an *apologia*.

"This record," she writes, "is a total work conceived graphically, musically, lyrically and accidentally—as a whole. The performances were guided by the given compositional structures and the audibly inspired beauty of every player. The whole unfolded like a mystery. It is not my intention to

Wilton Felder, and Joe Sample), with Chuck Findley on brass, and Bud Shank on saxophone and flute. Also present are the old, dear friends of the early days: Graham Nash, David Crosby, and James Taylor. Without them, it hardly would seem a Joni Mitchell recording.

It's a strange album, this one, detached, almost impersonal. Joni keeps her voice down in its lowest registers; the effect is less than impassioned and involving. The subject matter, of the song cycle—for song

unravel that mystery for anyone, but rather to offer some additional clues: 'Centerpiece' is a Johnny Mandel-Jon Hendricks tune. John Guerin and I collaborated on 'The Hissing of Summer Lawns.' 'The Boho Dance' is a Tom Wolfe-ism from the book 'The Painted Word.' The poem, 'Don't Interrupt the Sorrow,' was born around 4 a.m. in a New York loft. Larry Poons seeded it and Bobby Neuwirth was midwife here, but the child, filtered through Genesis at Jackfish Lake, Saskatchewan, is rebellious and mystical and insists that its conception was immaculate.

"Henry—more than an engineer—Lewy and his assistant Ellis Sorkin piloted these tapes to their destination; Henry and I mixed them; and Bernie Grundman mastered them at A&M studios in Hollywood. I drew the cover and designed the package with research help and guidance from Glen Christensen, Elektra/Asylum Art Director. The photo is Norman Seeff's. I would especially like to thank Myrt and Bill Anderson, North Battleford, New York, Saskatoon, Bel-Air, Burbank, Burundi, Orange County, the deep, deep heart of Dixie, Blue, National Geographic Magazine, Helpful Henry the Housewife's Delight—and John Guerin for showing me the root of the chord and where I was."

And, under a photograph of Joni floating lazily in a bikini, the water only partly submerging her, the words: "She could see the blue pools in the squinting sun and hear the hissing of summer lawns . . ." from the title song of the album.

The cover design is totally mystifying until one reads Joni's dedication-liner note. A group of what appears to be National Geographic Amazonian Indians (or Burundi natives?) drag a headless anaconda up a green lawn toward an urban-suburban collage of a landscape—part New York, part Saskatoon, and, down in the lower left corner of the jacket, the house in Bel-Air, complete with swimming pool.

"In France They Kiss on Main Street" leads off the album; a rollicking, rocking number, about dancing and necking and rebelling against parental suburban morality in the early sixties: "In the War of Independence Rock 'n' Roll rang sweet as victory," sings Joni, backed by Crosby, Nash, and Taylor. "Young love was kissing under bridges, kissing in cars, kissing in cafes." A total piece of nostalgia about a young girl who always loved to dance, Joni herself.

But "The Jungle Line" is something else again . . . something dark and misterioso, a song heavy with the jungle drums of Burundi and its references to the painter Rousseau, who painted primitive canvases of sleeping gypsies and stalking lions, and strange, luscious foliage. Rousseau in a jazz cellar where they drool "for a taste of something smuggled in," where poppy is poison and dues must be paid, where a working girl can be eaten alive. And, behind Joni's darkest voice, those pounding jungle drums of Burundi.

This is an album of contrasts—contrasts between shadows and light, blindness and sight, death and birth, and (in "Shades of Scarlet Conquering") a woman who is "cast iron and frail, with her impossibly gentle hands and her blood-red fingernails."

In the title song, where a woman is kept locked away like a "diamond dog" in a big ranch house on a hill by the man who has married her, who builds a barbed wire fence around her, the contrast is between her blindness (she carries "a cup and a cane") and the fact that she can look "thru a double glass . . . at too much pride and too much shame." And there is an ironic contrast between his holding her prisoner in darkness, and her own decision to stay "with a love of some kind. It's the lady's choice."

The most important song on the album, and the one that received most of the airplay, is "Harry's House—Centerpiece," in which Joni has combined the Mandel-Hendricks song with one of her own for dramatic effect. In story, it's the other side of "The Arrangement," a song about a man successful in worldly terms—in business—but a failure in his own life. Harry comes to New York City, where "skinny black models with raven curls, beauty parlor blondes with credit card eyes [are] looking for the chic and the fancy to buy." It is a city of success, where "battalions of paper-minded males, talking commodities and sales" have at home paper wives and paper kids who keep their "gut reactions hid." Unpacking, getting ready for his button-down business meetings, Harry remembers his wife as she was when he met her. "He drifts off into the memory of the way she looked in school, with her body oiled and shining at the public swimming pool . . ."

The song then cuts into "Centerpiece," a deeply romantic jazz ballad, about a boy and girl who fall in love and decide to marry because they can't live without each other. They will look for a little cottage on the outskirts . . . a far cry from the huge house

that successful Harry has managed to buy or build for his wife in the passing years.

Then, back to "Harry's House," and the final ironic twist—his wife has left him, and told him exactly what he could do with his house, his takehome pay, and his success. So much for the romantic dreams of young lovers.

It would be astonishing indeed if *The Hissing of Summer Lawns* reached the same pinnacle of success that *For the Roses* or *Court and Spark* did. It is so much less accessible . . . the songs are not singable by anybody but Joni . . . less melodic, less personally engaging. This album marks the emergence of a total new style for Joni, no longer on her Magic Princess trip. Still poetical, it has taken Joni away from her customary and very popular subject matter —the fragile nature of the heart and the complex byways it takes in its searches for another heart—and into avenues of expression that many of her listeners may be too perplexed to follow.

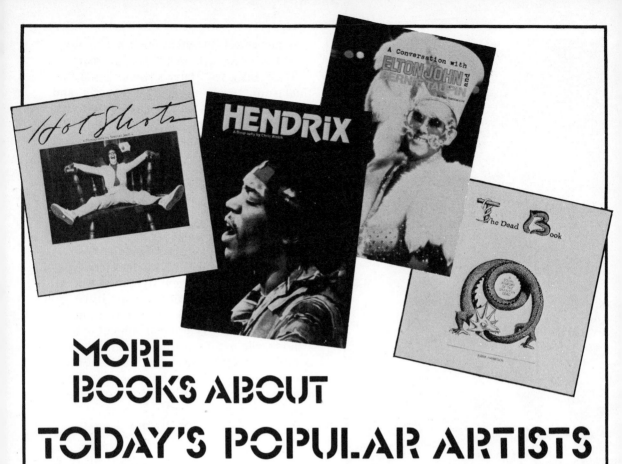

MORE BOOKS ABOUT TODAY'S POPULAR ARTISTS

Hot Shots
by Norman Seeff

This recipient of The One Show Gold Award for the best editorial photography in 1975 is a "series of definitive portraits featuring today's top stars" (*Penthouse*). These beautifully printed, black and white glossy images are by photographer Norman Seeff, who has known and photographed the "superstars" through the years of their emergence and stardom. Here then are the Stones, Patti Smith, The Band, Stevie Wonder, Joni Mitchell, Sly Stone, James Taylor, Andy Warhol and over 80 others. 96 pages, illustrated, $3.95

Hendrix
A Biography
by Chris Welch

This unsentimental but appreciative biography of the late superstar is full of not only facts, dates, names and places, but also some of the frankest interviews ever published, revealing Jimi as a musician, friend, lover, on-stage cut-up and off-stage human being. A wealth of photos illustrate Jimi's brief, blazing life, from his early days in Seattle coming up the hard way, through his years at the top of the heap.
104 pages, illustrated, $3.95

Elton John and Bernie Taupin
Edited by Paul Gambaccini

Here is the intimate portrait of a rock superstar in his own words and with exclusive personal and performance photos. In this unusual and revealing book, Elton John tells Paul Gambaccini of his not-so-easy rise to the top of the pop-music scene. He talks about his childhood, about studying at the Royal Academy, his first love, his work, and the famous personalities who inhabit his world. He tells, too, of his meeting with Bernie Taupin, who also shares many inside anecdotes about the music world and those who make it up. A discography of their albums is also included.
104 pages, illustrated, $3.95

The Dead Book
A Social History of the Grateful Dead
by Hank Harrison

"History of the Grateful Dead and of the California hip era of the 1960's. Well written in a flowing, acidy perception. Photos, drawings and tasteful design."—*Rock* Magazine

"It explains what we went through in the Haight and it captures the freedom and candor of it . . . I am really impressed with the research and the way the book moves, it's very stoney."—Jerry Garcia
180 pages, illustrated, $4.95